The Writings of Gregory Thaumaturgus

The Writings of Gregory Thaumaturgus

The Writings of Gregory Thaumaturgus

© Lighthouse Publishing 2023

Written by: Gregory Thaumaturgus (AD 213 - 270)
Translated by: Rev. S. D. F. Salmond, M.A. (1838-1905)
Updated into Modern U.S English: A.M. Overett (b.1960)

All rights reserved. Without limiting the rights under copyright reserved above, no part of this publication may be reproduced, stored in a retrieval system, or transmitted, in any form or by any means (electronic, mechanical, photocopying, recording or otherwise), without the prior written permission of the copyright owner of this book.

Published by
Lighthouse Publishing
SAN 257-4330
228 Freedom Parkway
Hoschton, GA 30548
United States of America

www.lighthousechristianpublishing.com

Introductory Note

To

Gregory Thaumaturgus.

[a.d. 205–240–265.] Alexandria continues to be the head of Christian learning. It is delightful to trace the hand of God from generation to generation, as from father to son, interposing for the perpetuity of the faith. We have already observed the continuity of the great Alexandrian school: how it arose, and how Pantænus begat Clement, and Clement begat Origen. So Origen begat Gregory, and so the Lord has provided for the spiritual generation of the Church's teachers, age after age, from the beginning. Truly, the Lord gave to Origen a holy seed, better than natural sons and daughters; as if, for his comfort, Isaiah had written, forbidding him to say, "I am a dry tree."

Our Gregory has given us not a little of his personal adventures in his panegyric upon his master, and for his further history the reader need only be referred to what follows. But I am anxious to supply the dates, which are too loosely left to conjecture. As he was ordained a bishop "very young," according to Eusebius, I suppose he must have been far enough under *fifty*, the age prescribed by the "Apostolic Canons" (so called), though probably not younger than *thirty*, the earliest canonical limit for the ordination of a presbyter. If we decide upon *five and thirty*, as a mean reckoning, we may with some confidence set his birth at a.d. 205, dating back from his episcopate, which began a.d. 240. He was a native of Neo-Cæsarea, the chief city of Pontus,—a fact that should modify what we have learned about Pontus from Tertullian. He was born of heathen parentage, and lived like other Gentile boys until his fourteenth year (*circa* a.d. 218), with the disadvantage of being more than ordinarily imbued by a mistaken father in the polytheism of Greece. At this period his father died; but his mother, carrying out the wishes of her husband, seems to have been not less zealous in furthering his education according to her pagan ideas. He was, evidently, the inheritor of moderate wealth; and, with his brother Athenodorus, he was placed under an accomplished teacher of grammar and rhetoric, from whom also he acquired a considerable knowledge of the Latin tongue. He was persuaded by the same master to use this accomplishment in acquiring some knowledge of the Roman laws. This is a very important point in his biography, and it brings us to an epoch in Christian history too little noted by any writer. I shall return to it very soon. We find him next going to Alexandria to study the New Platonism. He speaks of himself as already prepossessed with Christian ideas, which came to him even in his boyhood, about the time when his father died. But it was not at Alexandria that he began his acquaintance with Christian learning. Next he seems to have travelled into Greece, and to have studied at Athens. But the great interest of his autobiography begins with the providential incidents, devoutly narrated by himself, which engaged him in a journey to Berytus just as Origen reached Cæsarea, a.d. 233, making it for a time his home and the seat of his school. His own good angel, as Gregory supposes, led him away from Berytus, where he purposed to prosecute his legal studies, and brought him to the feet of Origen, his Gamaliel; and "from the very first day of his receiving us," he says, "the true Sun began to rise upon me." This he accounts the beginning of his true life; and, if we are right as to our dates, he was now about twenty-seven years of age.

If he tarried even a little while in Berytus, as seems probable, his knowledge of law was, doubtless, somewhat advanced. It was the seat of that school in which Roman law began its existence in the forms long afterward digested into the Pandects of Justinian. That emperor speaks of Berytus as "the mother and nurse" of the civil law. Caius, whose *Institutes* were discovered in 1820 by the sagacity of Niebuhr, seems to have been a Syrian. So were Papinian and Ulpian: and, heathen as they were, they lived under the illumination reflected from Antioch; and, not less than the Antonines, they were examples of a philosophic regeneration which never could have existed until the Christian era had begun its triumphs. Of this sort of pagan philosophy Julian became afterwards the grand embodiment; and in Julian's grudging confessions of what he had learned from Christianity we have a key to the secret convictions of others, such as I have named; characters in whom, as in Plutarch and in many retrograde unbelievers of our day, we detect the operation of influences they are unwilling to acknowledge; of which, possibly, they are blindly unconscious themselves. Roman law, I maintain, therefore, indirectly owes its origin, as it is directly indebted for its completion in the Pandects, to the new powers and processes of thought which came from "the Light of the World." It was light from Galilee and Golgotha, answering Pilate's question in the inward convictions of many a heathen sage.

It is most interesting, therefore, to find in our Gregory one who had come into contact with Berytus at this period. He describes it as already dignified by this school of law, and therefore Latinized in some degree by its influence. Most suggestive is what he says of this school: "I refer to those admirable laws *of our sages*, by which the affairs of all the subjects of the Roman Empire *are now* directed, and which are neither digested nor learnt without difficulty. They are wise and strict (if not *pious*) in themselves, they are manifold and admirable, and, in a word, *most thoroughly Grecian, although* expressed and delivered to us in the Roman tongue, which is a wonderful and magnificent sort of language, and one very aptly conformable to imperial authority, but still difficult to me." Nor is this the only noteworthy tribute of our author to Roman law while yet that sublime system was in its cradle. The rhetorician who introduced him to it and to the Latin tongue was its enthusiastic eulogist; and Gregory says he learned the laws "in a *thorough way,* by his help....And he said one thing to me which has proved to me the truest of all his sayings; to wit, that *my education in the laws* would be my greatest *viaticum,*—my ἐφόδιον (for thus he phrased it);" i.e., for the journey of life. This man, one can hardly doubt, was a disciple of Caius (or Gaius); and there is little question that the *digested* system which Gregory eulogizes was "the Institutes" of that great father of the civil law, now recovered from a palimpsest, and made known to our own age, with no less benefit to jurisprudence than the discovery of the *Philosophumena* has conferred on theology.

Thus Gregory's *Panegyric* throws light on the origin of Roman law. He claims it for "our sages," meaning men of the East, whose vernacular was the Greek tongue. Caius was probably, like the Gaius of Scripture, an Oriental who had borrowed a Latin name, as did the Apostle of the Gentiles and many others. If he was a native of Berytus, as seems probable, that ac- counts for the rise of the school of laws at a place comparatively inconsiderable. Hadrian, in his journey to Palestine, would naturally discover and patronize such a jurist; and that accounts for the appearance of Caius at Rome in his day. Papinian and Ulpian, both Orientals, were his pupils in all probability; and these were the "sages" with whose works the youthful Gregory became acquainted, and by which his mind was prepared for the great influence he exerted in the East, where his name is a power to this day.

His credit with our times is rather impaired than heightened by the epithet *Thaumaturgus*, which clings to his name as a convenient specification, to distinguish him from the other Gregories whose period was so nearly his own. But why make it his opprobrium? He is not responsible for the romances that sprung up after his death; which he never heard of nor imagined. Like the great Friar Bacon, who was considered a magician, or Faust, whose invention nearly cost him his life, the reputation of Gregory made him the subject of legendary lore long after he was gone. It is not impossible that God wrought marvels by his hand, but a single instance would give rise to many fables; and this very surname is of itself a monument of the fact that miracles were now of rare occurrence, and that one possessing the gift was a wonder to his contemporaries.

To like popular love of the marvelous I attribute the stupid story of a mock consecration by Phædimus. If a slight irregularity in Origen's ordination gave him such lifelong troubles, what would not have been the tumult such a sacrilege as this would have occasioned? Nothing is more probable than that Phædimus related such things as having occurred in a vision; and this might have weighed with a mind like Gregory's to overcome his scruples, and to justify his acceptance of such a position at an early age.

We are already acquainted with the eloquent letter of Origen that decided him to choose the sacred calling after he left the school at Cæsarea. The *Panegyric*, which was his valedictory, doubtless called forth that letter. Origen had seen in him the makings of a κῆρυξ, and coveted such another Timothy for the Master's work. But the *Panegyric* itself abounds with faults, and greatly resembles similar college performances of our day. The custom of schools alone can excuse the expression of such enthusiastic praise in the presence of its subject; but Origen doubtless bore it as philosophically as others have done since, and its evident sincerity and heartfelt gratitude redeem it from the charge of fulsome adulation.

For the residue of the story I may refer my readers to the statements of the translator, as follows:—

Translator's Notice.

We are in possession of a considerable body of testimonies from ancient literature bearing on the life and work of Gregory. From these, though they are largely mixed up with the marvelous, we gain a tolerably clear and satisfactory view of the main facts in his history, and the most patent features of his character. From various witnesses we learn that he was also known by the name Theodorus, which may have been his original designation; that he was a native of Neo-Cæsareia, a considerable place of trade, and one of the most important towns of Pontus; that he belonged to a family of some wealth and standing; that he was born of heathen parents; that at the age of fourteen he lost his father; that he had a brother named Athenodorus; and that along with him he travelled about from city to city in the prosecution of studies that were to fit him for the profession of law, to which he had been destined. Among the various seats of learning which he thus visited we find Alexandria, Athens, Berytus, and the Palestinian Cæsareia mentioned. At this last place— to which, as he tells us, he was led by a happy accident in the providence of God—he was brought into connection with Origen. Under this great teacher he received lessons in logic, geometry, physics, ethics, philosophy, and ancient literature, and in due time also in biblical science and the verities of the Christian faith. Thus, having become Origen's pupil, he became also by the hand of God his convert. After a residence of some five years with the great Alexandrian, he returned to his native city. Soon, however, a letter followed him to Neo-Cæsareia, in which Origen urged him to dedicate himself to the ministry of the Church of Christ, and pressed strongly upon him his obligation to consecrate his gifts to the service of God, and in especial to devote his acquirements in heathen science and learning to the elucidation of the Scriptures. On receipt of this letter, so full of wise and faithful counsel and strong exhortation, from the teacher whom he venerated and loved above all others, he withdrew into the wilderness, seeking opportunity for solemn thought and private prayer over its contents. At this time the bishop of Amasea, a city which held apparently a first place in the province, was one named Phædimus, who, discerning the promise of great things in the convert, sought to make him bishop of Neo-Cæsareia. For a considerable period, however, Gregory, who shrank from the responsibility of the episcopal office, kept himself beyond the bishop's reach, until Phædimus, unsuccessful in his search, had recourse to the stratagem of ordaining him in his absence, and declaring him, with all the solemnities of the usual ceremonial, bishop of his native city. On receiving the report of this extraordinary step, Gregory yielded, and, coming forth from the place of his concealment, was consecrated to the bishopric with all the customary formalities; and so well did he discharge the duties of his office, that while there were said to be only seventeen Christians in the whole city when he first entered it as bishop, there were said to be only seventeen pagans in it at the time of his death. The date of his studies under Origen is fixed at about 234 a.d., and that of his ordination as bishop at about 240. About the year 250 his church was involved in the sufferings of the Decian persecution, on which occasion he fled into the wilderness, with the hope of pre- serving his life for his people, whom he also counselled to follow in that matter his example. His flock had much to endure, again, through the incursion of the northern barbarians about 260. He took part in the council that met at Antioch in 265 for the purpose of trying Paul of Samosata; and soon after that he died, perhaps about 270, if we can adopt the conjectural reading which gives the name Aurelian instead of Julian in the account left us by Suidas.

The surname Thaumaturgus, or *Wonder-worker*, at once admonishes us of the *marvelous* that so largely connected itself with the *historical* in the ancient records of this man's life. He was believed to have been gifted with a power of working miracles, which he was constantly exercising. But into these it is profitless to enter. When all the marvelous is dissociated from the historical in the records of this bishop's career, we have still the figure of a great, good, and gifted man, deeply versed in the heathen lore and science of his time, yet more deeply imbued with the genuine spirit of another wisdom, which, under God, he learned from the illustrious thinker of Alexandria, honoring with all love, gratitude, and veneration that teacher to whom he was indebted for his knowledge of the Gospel, and exercising an earnest, enlightened, and faithful ministry of many years in an office which he had not sought, but for which he had been sought. Such is, in brief, the picture that rises up before us from a perusal of his own writings, as well as from the comparison of ancient accounts of the man and his vocation. Of his well-accredited works we have the following: *A Declaration of Faith*, being a creed on the doctrine of the Trinity; a *Metaphrase of the Book of Ecclesiastes*, a *Panegyric to Origen*, being an oration delivered on leaving the school of Origen, expressing eloquently, and with great tenderness of feeling, as well as polish of style, the sense of his obligations to that master; and a *Canonical Epistle*, in which he gives a variety of directions with respect to the penances and discipline to be exacted by the Church from Christians who had fallen back into heathenism in times of suffering, and wished to be re- stored. Other works have been attributed to him, which are doubtful or spurious. His writings have been often edited,—by Gerard Voss in 1604, by the Paris editors in 1662, by Gallandiin 1788, and others, who need not be enumerated here.

Part I.—Acknowledged Writings.

A Declaration of Faith.

There is one God, the Father of the living Word, *who is His* subsistent Wisdom and Power and Eternal Image: perfect Begetter of the perfect *Begotten*, Father of the only-begotten Son. There is one Lord, Only of the Only, God of God, Image and Likeness of Deity, Efficient Word, Wisdom comprehensive of the constitution of all things, and Power formative of the whole creation, true Son of true Father, Invisible of Invisible, and Incorruptible of Incorruptible, and Immortal of Immortal and Eternal of Eternal. And there is One Holy Spirit, having His subsistence from God, and being made manifest by the Son, to wit to men: Image of the Son, Perfect *Image* of the Perfect; Life, the Cause of the living; Holy Fount; Sanctity, the Supplier, *or Leader*, of Sanctification; in whom is manifested God the Father, who is above all and in all, and God the Son, who is through all. There is a perfect Trinity, in glory and eternity and sovereignty, neither divided nor estranged. Wherefore there is nothing either created or in servitude in the Trinity; nor anything superinduced, as if at some former period it was non-existent, and at some later period it was introduced. And thus neither was the Son ever wanting to the Father, nor the Spirit to the Son; but without variation and without change, the same Trinity *abides* ever.

Elucidation.

The story of the "Revelation" is of little consequence, though, if this were Gregory's genuine work, it would be easy to account for it as originating in a beautiful dream. But it is very doubtful whether it be a genuine work; and, to my mind, it is most fairly treated by Lardner, to whose elaborate chapter concerning Gregory every scholar must refer. Dr. Burton, in his edition of Bishop Bull's works, almost overrules that learned prelate's inclination to think it genuine, in the following words: "Hanc formulam minime esse Gregorii authenticam...multis *haud spernendis argumentis demonstrat* Lardner." Lardner thinks it a fabrication of the fourth century.

Cave's learned judgment is more favorable; and he gives the text from Gregory of Nyssa, which he translates as follows: "There is one God, the Father of the living Word and of the subsisting Wisdom and Power, and of Him who is His Eternal Image, the perfect be- getter of Him that is perfect, the Father of the only-begotten Son. There is one Lord, the only *Son* of the only *Father*, God of God, the character and image of the Godhead, the powerful Word, the comprehensive Wisdom, by which all things were made, and the Power that gave being to the whole creation, the true Son of the true Father, the Invisible of the Invisible, the Incorruptible of the Incorruptible, the Immortal of the Immortal, and the Eternal of Him that is Eternal. There is one Holy Ghost, having its subsistence of God, which appeared through the Son to mankind, the perfect Image of the perfect Son, the

Life-giving Life, the holy Fountain, the Sanctity, and the Author of sanctification, by whom God the Father is made manifest, who is over all, and in all; and God the Son, who is through all. A perfect Trinity, which neither in glory, eternity, or dominion is divided, or departed from itself."

A Metaphrase of the Book of Ecclesiastes

Chapter I.

These words speaks Solomon, the son of David the king and prophet, to the whole Church of God, a prince most honored, and a prophet most wise above all men. How vain and fruitless are the affairs of men, and all pursuits that occupy man! For there is not one who can tell of any profit attaching to those things which men who creep on earth strive by body and soul to attain to, in servitude all the while to what is transient, and undesirous of considering aught heavenly with the noble eye of the soul. And the life of men wears away, as day by day, and in the periods of hours and years, and the determinate courses of the sun, some are ever coming, and others passing away. And the matter is like the transit of torrents as they fall into the measureless deep of the sea with a mighty noise. And all things that have been constituted by God for the sake of men abide the same: as, for instance, that man is born of earth, and departs to earth again; that the earth itself continues stable; that the sun accomplishes its circuit about it perfectly, and rolls round to the same mark again; and that the winds in like manner, and the mighty rivers which flow into the sea, and the breezes that beat upon it, all act without forcing it to pass beyond its limits, and without themselves also violating their appointed laws. And these things, indeed, as bearing upon the good of this life of ours, are established thus fittingly. But those things which are of men's devising, whether words or deeds, have no measure. And there is a plenteous multitude of words, but there is no profit from random and foolish talking. But the race of men is naturally insatiate in its thirst both for speaking and for hearing what is spoken; and it is man's habit, too, to desire to look with idle eyes on all that happens. What can occur afterwards, or what can be wrought by men which has not been done already? What new thing is there worthy of mention, of which there has never yet been experience? For I think there is nothing which one may call new, or which, on considering it, one shall discover to be strange or unknown to those of old. But as former things are buried in oblivion, so also things that are now subsistent will in the course of time vanish utterly from the knowledge of those who shall come after us. And I speak not these things unadvisedly, as acting now the preacher. But all these things were carefully pondered by me when entrusted with the kingdom of the Hebrews in Jerusalem. And I examined diligently, and considered discreetly, the nature of all that is on earth, and I perceived it to be most various; *and I saw* that to man it is given to labor upon earth, ever carried about by all different occasions of toil, and with no result of his work. And all things here below are full of the spirit of strangeness and abomination, so that it is not possible for one to retrieve them now; nay, rather it is not possible for one at all to conceive what utter vanity has taken possession of all human affairs. For once on a time I communed with myself, and thought that then I was wiser in this than all that were before me, and I was expert in understanding parables and the natures of things. But I learned that I gave myself to such pursuits to no purpose, and that if wisdom follows knowledge, so troubles attend on wisdom.

Chapter II.

Judging, therefore, that it stood thus with this matter, I decided to turn to another manner of life, and to give myself to pleasure, and to take experience of various delights. And now I learned that all such things are vain; and I put a check on laughter, when it ran on carelessly; and restrained pleasure, according to the rule of moderation, and was bitterly wroth against it. And when I perceived that the soul is able to arrest the body in its disposition to intoxication and winebibbing, and that temperance makes lust its subject, I sought earnestly to observe what object of true worth and of real excellence is set before men, which they shall attain to in this present life. For I passed through all those other objects which are deemed worthiest, such as the erecting of lofty houses and the planting of vines, and in addition, the laying out of pleasure-grounds, and the acquisition and culture of all manner of fruit-bearing trees; and among them also large reservoirs for the reception of water were constructed, and distributed so as to secure the plentiful irrigation of the trees. And I sur- rounded myself also with many domestics, both manservants and maid-servants; and some of them I procured from abroad, and others I possessed and employed as born in my own house. And herds of four-footed creatures, as well of cattle as of sheep, more numerous than any of those of old acquired, were made my property. And treasures of gold and silver flowed in upon me; and I made the kings of all nations my dependents and tributaries. And very many choirs of male and female singers were trained to yield me pleasure by the practice of all-harmonious song. And I had banquetings; and for the service of this part of my pleasure, I got me select cup-bearers of both sexes beyond my reckoning,—so far did I surpass in these things those who reigned before me in Jerusalem. And thus it happened that the interests of wisdom declined with me, while the claims of evil appetency increased. For when I yielded myself to every allurement of the eyes, and to the violent passions of the heart, that make their attack from all quarters, and surrendered myself to the hopes held out by pleasures, I also made my will the bond-slave of all miserable delights. For thus my judgment was brought to such a wretched pass, that I thought these things good, and that it was proper for me to engage in them. At length, awaking and recovering my sight, I perceived that the things I had in hand were altogether sinful and very evil, and the deeds of a spirit not good. For now none of all the objects of men's choice seem to me worthy of approval, or greatly to be desired by a just mind. Wherefore, having pondered at once the advantages of wisdom and the ills of folly, I should with reason admire that man greatly, who, being borne on in a thoughtless course, and afterwards arresting himself, should return to right and duty. For wisdom and folly are widely separated, and they are as different from each other as day is from night. He, therefore, who makes choice of virtue, is like one who sees all things plainly, and looks upward, and who holds his ways in the time of clearest light. But he, on the other hand, who has involved himself in wickedness, is like a man who wanders helplessly about in a moonless night, as one who is blind, and deprived of the sight of things by his darkness. And when I considered the end of each of these modes of life, I found there was no profit in the latter; and by setting myself to be the companion of the foolish, I saw that I should receive the wages of folly. For what advantage is there in those thoughts, or what profit is there in the multitude of words, where the streams of foolish speaking are flowing, as it were, from the fountain of folly? Moreover, there is nothing common to the wise man and to the fool, neither as regards the memory of men, nor as regards the recompense of God. And as to all the affairs of men, when they are yet apparently but beginning to be, the end at once surprises them. Yet the wise man is never partaker of the same end with the foolish. Then also did I hate all my life, that had been consumed in vanities, and which I had spent with a mind engrossed in earthly anxieties. For, to speak in brief, all my affairs have been wrought by me with labor and pain, as the efforts of thoughtless impulse; and some other person, it may be a wise man or a fool, will succeed to them, I mean, the chill fruits of my toils. But when I cut myself off from these things, and cast them away, then did that real good which is set before man show itself to me,—namely, the knowledge of wisdom and the possession of manly virtue. And if a man neglects these things, and is inflamed with the passion for other things, such a man makes choice of evil instead of good, and goes after what is bad instead of what is excellent, and after trouble instead of peace; for he is distracted by every manner of disturbance, and is burdened with continual anxieties night and day, with oppressive labors of body as well as with ceaseless cares of mind,—his heart moving in constant agitation, by reason of the strange and senseless affairs that occupy him. For the perfect good does not consist in eating and drinking, although it is true that it is from God that their sustenance cometh to men; for none of those things which are given for our maintenance subsist without His providence. But the good man who gets wisdom from God, gets also heavenly enjoyment; while, on the other hand, the evil man, smitten with ills divinely inflicted, and afflicted with the disease of lust, toils to amass much, and is quick to put him to shame who is honored by God in presence of the Lord of all, proffering useless gifts, and making things deceitful and vain the pursuits of his own miserable soul.

Chapter III.

For this present time is filled with all things that are most contrary to each other—births and deaths, the growth of plants and their uprooting, cures and killings, the building up and the pulling down of houses, weeping and laughing, mourning and dancing. At this moment a man gathers of earth's products, and at another casts them away; and at one time he ardently desires *the beauty of* woman, and at another he hates it. Now he seeks something, and again he loses it; and now he keeps, and again he casted away; at one time he slayed, and at another he is slain; he speaks, and again he is silent; he loved, and again he hated. For the affairs of men are at one time in a condition of war, and at another in a condition of peace; while their fortunes are so inconstant, that from bearing the semblance of good, they change quickly into acknowledged ills. Let us have done, therefore, with vain labors. For all these things, as appears to me, are set to madden men, as it were, with their poisoned stings. And the ungodly observer of the times and seasons is agape for this world, exerting himself above measure to destroy the image of God, as one who has chosen to contend against it from the beginning onward to the end. I am persuaded, therefore, that the greatest good for man is cheerfulness and well-doing, and that this short-lived enjoyment, which alone is possible to us, comes from God only, if righteousness direct our doings. But as to those everlasting and incorruptible things which God hath firmly established, it is not possible either to take aught from them or to add ought to them. And to men in general, those things, in sooth, are fearful and wonderful; and those things indeed which have been, abide so; and those which are to be, have already been, as regards His foreknowledge. Moreover, the man who is injured has God as his helper. I saw in the lower parts the pit of punishment which receives the impious, but a different place allotted for the pious. And I thought with myself, that with God all things are judged and determined to be equal; that the righteous and the unrighteous, and objects with reason and without reason, are alike in His judgment. For that their time is measured out equally to all, and death impends over them, and *in this* the races of beasts and men are alike in the judgment of God, and differ from each other only in the matter of articulate speech; and all things else happen alike to them, and death receives all equally, not more so in the case of the other kinds of creatures than in that of men. For they have all the same breath *of life*, and men have nothing more; but all are, in one word, vain, deriving their present condition from the same earth, and destined to perish, and return to the same earth again. For it is uncertain regarding the souls of men, whether they shall fly upwards; and regarding the others which the unreasoning creatures possess, whether they shall fall downward. And it seemed to me, that there is no other good save pleasure, and the enjoyment of things present. For I did not think it possible for a man, when once he has tasted death, to return again to the enjoyment of these things.

Chapter IV.

And leaving all these reflections, I considered and turned in aversion from all the forms of oppression which are done among men; whence some receiving injury weep and lament, who are struck down by violence in utter default of those who protect them, or who should by all means comfort them in their trouble. And the men who make might their right are exalted to an eminence, from which, however, they shall also fall. Yea, of the unrighteous and audacious, those who are dead fare better than those who are still alive. And better than both these is he who, being destined to be like them, has not yet come into being, since he has not yet touched the wickedness which prevails among men. And it became clear to me also how great is the envy which follows a man from his neighbors, like the sting of a wicked spirit; and *I saw* that he who receives it, and takes it as it were into his breast, has nothing else but to eat his own heart, and tear it, and consume both soul and body, finding inconsolable vexation in the good fortune of others. And a wise man would choose to have one of his hands full, if it were with ease and quietness, rather than both of them with travail and with the villainy of a treacherous spirit. Moreover, there is yet another thing which I know to happen contrary to what is fitting, by reason of the evil will of man. He who is left entirely alone, having neither brother nor son, but prospered with large possessions, lives on in the spirit of insatiable avarice, and refuses to give himself in any way whatever to goodness. Gladly, therefore, would I ask such a one for what reason he labors thus, fleeing with headlong speed from the doing of anything good, and distracted by the many various passions for making gain. Far better than such are those who have taken up an order of life in common, from which they may reap the best blessings. For when two men devote themselves in the right spirit to the same objects, though some mischance befalls the one, he has still at least no slight alleviation in having his companion by him. And the greatest of all calamities to a man in evil fortune is the want of a friend to help and cheer him. And those who live together both double the good fortune that befalls them, and lessen the pressure of the storm of disagreeable events; so that in the day they are distinguished for their frank confidence in each other, and in the night they appear notable for their cheerful- ness.[65] But he who leads a solitary life passes a species of existence full of terror to himself; not perceiving that if one should fall upon men welded closely together, he adopts a rash and perilous course, and that it is not easy to snap the threefold cord. Moreover, I put a poor youth, if he be wise, before an aged prince devoid of wisdom, to whose thoughts it has never occurred that it is possible that a man may be raised from the prison to the throne, and that the very man who has exercised his power unrighteously shall at a later period be righteously cast out. For it may happen that those who are subject to a youth, who is at the same time sensible, shall be free from trouble,—those, I mean, who are his elders. Moreover, they who are born later cannot praise another, of whom they have had no experience, and are led by an unreasoning judgment, and by the impulse of a contrary spirit. But in exercising the preacher's office, keep thou this before thine eyes, that thine own life be rightly directed, and that thou prays on behalf of the foolish, that they may get understanding, and know how to shun the doings of the wicked.

Chapter V.

Moreover, it is a good thing to use the tongue sparingly, and to keep a calm and rightly balanced heart in the exercise of speech. For it is not right to give utterance in words to things that are foolish and absurd, or to all that occur to the mind; but we ought to know and reflect, that though we are far separated from heaven, we speak in the hearing of God, and that it is good for us to speak without offense. For as dreams and visions of many kinds attend manifold cares of mind, so also silly talking is conjoined with folly. Moreover, see to it, that a promise made with a vow be made good in fact. This, too, is proper to fools, that they are unreliable. But be thou true to thy word, knowing that it is much better for thee not to vow or promise to do anything, than to vow and then fail of performance. And thou oughtest by all means to avoid the flood of base words, seeing that God will hear them. For the man who makes such things his study gets no more benefit by them than to see his doings brought to nought by God. For as the multitude of dreams is vain, so also the multitude of words. But the fear of God is man's salvation, though it is rarely found. Wherefore thou oughtest not to wonder though thou sees the poor oppressed, and the judges misinterpreting the law. But thou oughtest to avoid the appearance of surpassing those who are in power. For even should this prove to be the case, yet, from the terrible ills that shall befall thee, wickedness of itself will not deliver thee. But even as property acquired by violence is a most hurtful as well as impious possession, so the man who lusted after money never finds satisfaction for his passion, nor good-will from his neighbors, even though he may have amassed the greatest possible wealth. For this also is vanity. But goodness greatly rejoices those who hold by it, and makes them strong, imparting to them the capacity of seeing through all things. And it is a great matter also not to be engrossed by such anxieties: for the poor man, even should he be a slave, and unable to fill his belly plentifully, enjoys at least the kind refreshment of sleep; but the lust of riches is attended by sleepless nights and anxieties of mind. And what could there be then more absurd, than with much anxiety and trouble to amass wealth, and keep it with jealous care, if all the while one is but maintaining the occasion of countless evils to himself? And this wealth, besides, must needs perish some time or other, and be lost, whether he who has acquired it has children or not; himself, however unwillingly, is doomed to die, and return to earth in the selfsame condition in which it was his lot once to come into being. And the fact that he is destined thus to leave earth with empty hands, will make the evil all the sorer to him, as he fails to consider that an end is appointed for his life similar to its beginning, and that he toils to no profit, and labors rather for the wind, as it were, than for the advancement of his own real interest, wasting his whole life in most unholy lusts and irrational passions, and withal in troubles and pains. And, to speak shortly, his days are darkness to such a man, and his life is sorrow. Yet this is in itself good, and by no means to be despised. For it is the gift of God, that a man should be able to reap with gladness of mind the fruits of his labors, receiving thus possessions bestowed by God, and not acquired by force. For neither is such a man afflicted with troubles, nor is he for the most part the slave of evil thoughts; but he measures out his life by good deeds, being of good heart in all things, and rejoicing in the gift of God.

Chapter VI.

Moreover, I shall exhibit in discourse the ill-fortune that most of all prevails among men. While God may supply a man with all that is according to his mind, and deprive him of no object which may in any manner appeal to his desires, whether it be wealth, or honor, or any other of those things for which men distract themselves; yet the man, while thus prospered in all things, as though the only ill inflicted on him from heaven were just the inability to enjoy them, may but husband them for his fellow, and fall without profit either to himself or to his neighbors. This I reckon to be a strong proof and clear sign of surpassing evil. The man who has borne without blame the name of father of very many children, and spent a long life, and has not had his soul filled with good for so long time, and has had no experience of death meanwhile,— this man I should not envy either his numerous offspring or his length of days; nay, I should say that the untimely birth that falls from a woman's womb is better than he.

For as that came in with vanity, so it also departed secretly in oblivion, without having tasted the ills of life or looked on the sun. And this is a lighter evil than for the wicked man not to know what is good, even though he measures his life by thousands of years. And the end of both is death. The fool is proved above all things by his finding no satisfaction in any lust. But the discreet man is not held captive by these passions. Yet, for the most part, righteousness of life leads a man to poverty. And the sight of curious eyes deranges many, inflaming their mind, and drawing them on to vain pursuits by the empty desire of show. Moreover, the things which are now are known already; and it becomes apparent that man is unable to contend with those that are above him. And, verily, inanities have their course among men, which only increase the folly of those who occupy themselves with them.

Chapter VII.

For though a man should be by no means greatly advantaged by knowing all in this life that is destined to befall him according to his mind (let us suppose such a case), nevertheless with the officious activity of men he devises means for prying into and gaining an apparent acquaintance with the things that are to happen after a person's death. Moreover, a good name is more pleasant to the mind than oil to the body; and the end of life is better than the birth, and to mourn is more desirable than to revel, and to be with the sorrowing is better than to be with the drunken. For this is the fact that he who comes to the end of life has no further care about aught around him. And discreet anger is to be preferred to laughter; for by the severe disposition of countenance the soul is kept upright. The souls of the wise, indeed, are sad and downcast, but those of fools are elated, and given loose to merriment. And yet it is far more desirable to receive blame from one wise man, than to become a hearer of a whole chorus of worthless and miserable men in their songs. For the laughter of fools is like the crackling of many thorns burning in a fierce fire. This, too, is misery, yea the greatest of evils, namely oppression; for it intrigues against the souls of the wise, and attempts to ruin the noble way of life which the good pursue. Moreover, it is right to commend not the man who begins, but the man who finishes a speech; and what is moderate ought to approve itself to the mind, and not what is swollen and inflated. Again, one ought certainly to keep wrath in check, and not suffer himself to be carried rashly into anger, the slaves of which are fools. Moreover, they are in error who assert that a better manner of life was given to those before us, and they fail to see that wisdom is widely different from mere abundance of possessions, and that it is as much more lustrous than these, as silver shines more brightly than its shadow. For the life of man hath its excellence not in the acquisition of perishable riches, but in wisdom. And who shall be able, tell me, to declare the providence of God, which is so great and so beneficent? or who shall be able to recall the things which seem to have been passed by of God? And in the former days of my vanity I considered all things, *and saw* a righteous man continuing in his righteousness, and ceasing not from it until death, but even suffering injury by reason thereof, and a wicked man perishing with his wickedness. Moreover, it is proper that the righteous man should not seem to be so overmuch, nor exceedingly and above measure wise, that he may not, as in making some slip, *seem to* sin many times over. And be not thou audacious and precipitate, lest an untimely death surprise thee. It is the greatest of all good to take hold of God, and by abiding in Him to sin in nothing. For to touch things undefiled with an impure hand is abomination. But he who in the fear of God submits himself, escapes all that is contrary. Wisdom availed more in the way of help than a band of the most powerful men in a city, and it often also pardons righteously those who fail in duty. For there is not one that stumbles not. Also it becomes thee in no way to attend upon the words of the impious, that thou mayest not become an ear-witness of words spoken against thyself, such as the foolish talk of a wicked servant, and being thus stung in heart, have recourse afterward thyself to cursing in turn in many actions. And all these things have I known, having received wisdom from God, which afterward I lost, and was no longer able to be the same. For wisdom fled from me to an infinite distance, and into a measureless depth, so that I could no longer get hold of it. Wherefore afterwards I abstained altogether from seeking it; and I no longer thought of considering the follies and the vain counsels of the impious, and their weary, distracted life. And being thus disposed, I was borne on to the things themselves; and being seized with a fatal passion, I knew woman— that she is like a snare or some such other object. For her heart ensnares those who pass her; and if she but joins hand to hand, she holds one as securely as though she dragged him on bound with chains. And from her you can secure your deliverance only by finding a propitious and watchful superintendent in God; for he who is enslaved by sin cannot (otherwise) escape its grasp. Moreover, among all women I sought for the chastity proper to them, and I found it in none. And verily a person may find one man chaste among a thousand, but a woman never. And this above all things I observed that men being made by God simple in mind, contract for themselves manifold reasonings and infinite questionings, and while professing to seek wisdom, waste their life in vain words.

Chapter VIII.

Moreover, wisdom, when it is found in a man, shows itself also in its possessor's face, and makes his countenance to shine; as, on the other hand, effrontery convicts the man in whom it has taken up its abode, so soon as he is seen, as one worthy of hatred. And it is on every account right to give careful heed to the words of the king, and by all manner of means to avoid an oath, especially one taken in the name of God. It may be fit at the same time to notice an evil word, but then it is necessary to guard against any blasphemy against God. For it will not be possible to find fault with Him when He inflicts any penalty, nor to gainsay the decrees of the Only Lord and King. But it will be better and more profitable for a man to abide by the holy commandments, and to keep himself apart from the words of the wicked. For the wise man knows and discerned beforehand the judgment, which shall come at the right time, and sees that it shall be just. For all things in the life of men await the retribution from above; but the wicked man does not seem to know verily that as there is a mighty providence over him, nothing in the future shall be hid. He knows not indeed the things which shall be; for no man shall be able to announce any one of them to him duly: for no one shall be found so strong as to be able to prevent the angel who spoils him of his life; neither shall any means be devised for canceling in any way the appointed time of death. But even as the man who is captured in the midst of the battle can only see flight cut off on every side, so all the impiety of man perishes utterly together. And I am astonished, as often as I contemplate what and how great things men have studied to do for the hurt of their neighbors. But this I know, that the impious are snatched prematurely from this life, and put out of the way because they have given themselves to vanity. For whereas the providential judgment of God does not overtake all speedily, by reason of His great long-suffering, and the wicked is not punished immediately on the commission of his offences,—for this reason he thinks that he may sin the more, as though he were to get off with impunity, not understanding that the transgressor shall not escape the knowledge of God even after a long interval. This, moreover, is the chief good, to reverence God; for if once the impious man falls away from Him, he shall not be suffered long to misuse his own folly. But a most vicious and false opinion often prevails among men concerning both the righteous and the unrighteous. For they form a judgment contrary to truth regarding each of them; and the man who is really righteous does not get the credit of being so, while, on the other hand, the impious man is deemed prudent and upright. And this I judge to be among the most grievous of errors. Once, indeed, I thought that the chief good consisted in eating and drinking, and that he was most highly favored of God who should enjoy these things to the utmost in his life; and I fancied that this kind of enjoyment was the only comfort in life. And, accordingly, I gave heed to nothing but to this conceit, so that neither by night nor by day did I withdraw myself from all those things which have ever been discovered to minister luxurious delights to men. And this much I learned thereby that the man who mingles in these things shall by no means be able, however sorely he may labor with them, to find the real good.

Chapter IX.

Now I thought at that time that all men were judged worthy of the same things. And if any wise man practiced righteousness, and withdrew himself from unrighteousness, and as being sagacious avoided hatred with all (which, indeed, is a thing well pleasing to God), this man seemed to me to labor in vain. For there seemed to be one end for the righteous and for the impious, for the good and for the evil, for the pure and for the impure, for him that worshipped God, and for him that worshipped not. For as the unrighteous man and the good, the man who swears a false oath, and the man who avoids swearing altogether, were suspected by me to be driving toward the same end, a certain sinister opinion stole secretly into my mind, that all men come to their end in a similar way. But now I know that these are the reflections of fools, and errors and deceits. And they assert largely, that he who is dead has perished utterly, and that the living is to be preferred to the dead, even though he may lie in darkness, and pass his life-journey after the fashion of a dog, *which is* better at least than a dead lion. For the living know this at any rate, that they are to die; but the dead know not anything, and there is no reward proposed to them after they have completed their necessary course. Also hatred and love with the dead have their end; for their envy has perished, and their life also is extinguished. And he has a portion in nothing who has once gone hence. Error harping still on such a string, gives also such counsel as this: What meanest thou, O man, that thou dost not enjoy thyself delicately, and gorge thyself with all manner of pleasant food, and fill thyself to the full with wine? Dost thou not perceive that these things are given us from God for our unrestrained enjoyment? Put on newly washed attire, and anoint thy head with myrrh, and see this woman and that, and pass thy vain life vainly. For nothing else remained for thee but this, neither here nor after death. But avail thou thyself of all that chances; for neither shall anyone take account of thee for these things, nor are the things that are done by men known at all outside the circle of men. And Hades, whatever that may be, whereunto we are said to depart, has neither wisdom nor understanding. These are the things which men of vanity speak. But I know assuredly that neither shall they who seem the swiftest accomplish that great race; nor shall those who are esteemed mighty and terrible in the judgment of men, overcome in that terrible battle. Neither, again, is prudence proved by abundance of bread, nor is understanding wont to consort with riches. Nor do I congratulate those who think that all shall find the same things befall them. But certainly, those who indulge such thoughts seem to me to be asleep, and to fail to consider that, caught suddenly like fishes and birds, they will be consumed with woes, and meet speedily their proper retribution. Also I estimate wisdom at so high a price, that I should deem a small and poorly peopled city, even though besieged also by a mighty king with his forces, to be indeed great and powerful, if it had but one wise man, however poor, among its citizens. For such a man would be able to deliver his city both from enemies and from entrenchments. And other men, it may be, do not recognize that wise man, poor as he is; but for my part I greatly prefer the power that resides in wisdom, to this might of the mere multitude of the people. Here, however, wisdom, as it dwells with poverty, is held in dishonor. But hereafter it shall be heard speaking with more authoritative voice than princes and despots who seek after things evil. For wisdom is also stronger than iron; while the folly of one individual works danger for many, even though he be an object of contempt to many.

Chapter X.

Moreover, flies falling into myrrh, and suffocated therein, make both the appearance of that pleasant ointment and the anointing therewith an unseemly thing; and to be mindful of wisdom and of folly together is in no way proper. The wise man, indeed, is his own leader to right actions; but the fool inclines to erring courses, and will never make his folly available as a guide to what is noble. Yea, his thoughts also are vain and full of folly. But if ever a hostile spirit falls upon thee, my friend, withstand it courageously, knowing that God is able to propitiate even a mighty multitude of offences. These also are the deeds of the prince and father of all wickedness: that the fool is set on high, while the man richly gifted with wisdom is humbled; and that the slaves of sin are seen riding on horseback, while men dedicated to God walk on foot in dishonor, the wicked exulting the while. But if anyone devises another's hurt, he forgets that he is preparing a snare for himself first and alone. And he who wrecks another's safety, shall fall by the bite of a serpent. But he who removes stones, indeed shall undergo no light labor; and he who cleaves wood shall bear danger with him in his own weapon. And if it chance that the axe springs out of the handle, he who engages in such work shall be put to trouble, gathering for no good and having to put to more of his iniquitous and short-lived strength. The bite of a serpent, again, is stealthy; and the charmers will not soothe the pain, for they are vain. But the good man doeth good works for himself and for his neighbors alike; while the fool shall sink into destruction through his folly. And when he has once opened his mouth, he begins foolishly and soon comes to an end, exhibiting his senselessness in all. Moreover, it is impossible for man to know anything, or to learn from man either what has been from the beginning, or what shall be in the future. For whom shall be the declarer thereof? Besides, the man who knows not to go to the good city, sustains evil in the eyes and in the whole countenance. And I prophesy woes to that city the king of which is a youth, and its ruler's gluttons. But I call the good land blessed, the king of which is the son of the free: there those who are entrusted with the power of ruling shall reap what is good in due season. But the sluggard and the idler become scoffers, and make the house decay; and misusing all things for the purposes of their own gluttony, like the ready slaves of money, for a small price they are content to do all that is base and abject. It is also right to obey kings and rulers or potentates, and not to be bitter against them, nor to utter any offensive word against them. For there is ever the risk that what has been spoken in secret may somehow become public. For swift and winged messengers convey all things to Him who alone is King both rich and mighty, discharging therein a service which is at once spiritual and reasonable.

Chapter XI.

Moreover, it is a righteous thing to give (to the needy) of thy bread, and of those things which are necessary for the support of man's life. For though thou seems forthwith to waste it upon some persons, as if thou didst cast thy bread upon the water, yet in the progress of time thy kindness shall be seen to be not unprofitable for thee. Also give liberally, and give a portion of thy means to many; for thou knows not what the coming day doeth. The clouds, again, do not keep back their plenteous rains, but discharge their showers upon the earth. Nor does a tree stand for ever; but even though men may spare it, it shall be overturned by the wind at any rate. But many desire also to know beforehand what is to come from the heavens; and there have been those who, scrutinizing the clouds and waiting for the wind, have had nought to do with reaping and winnowing, putting their trust in vanity, and being all incapable of knowing aught of what may come from God in the future; just as men cannot tell what the woman with child shall bring forth. But sow thou in season, and thus reap thy fruits whenever the time for that comes on. For it is not manifest what shall be better than those among all natural things. Would, indeed, that all things turned out well! Truly, when a man considers with himself that the sun is good, and that this life is sweet, and that it is a pleasant thing to have many years wherein one can delight himself continually, and that death is a terror and an endless evil, and a thing that brings us to nought, he thinks that he ought to enjoy himself in all the present and apparent pleasures of life. And he gives this counsel also to the young, that they should use to the uttermost the season of their youth, by giving up their minds to all manner of pleasure, and indulge their passions, and do all that seemed good in their own eyes, and look upon that which delighted, and avert themselves from that which is not so. But to such a man I shall say this much: Senseless art thou, my friend, in that thou dost not look for the judgment that shall come from God upon all these things. And profligacy and licentiousness are evil, and the filthy wantonness of our bodies carries death in it. For folly attends on youth, and folly leads to destruction.

Chapter XII.

Moreover, it is right that thou shouldest fear God while thou art yet young, before thou gives thyself over to evil things, and before the great and terrible day of God cometh, when the sun shall no longer shine, neither the moon, nor the rest of the stars, but when in that storm and commotion of all things, the powers above shall be moved, that is, the angels who guard the world; so that the mighty men shall fail, and the women shall cease their labors and shall flee into the dark places of their dwellings, and shall have all the doors shut. And a woman shall be restrained from grinding by fear, and shall speak with the weakest voice, like the tiniest bird; and all the impure women shall sink into the earth; and cities and their blood-stained governments shall wait for the vengeance that comes from above, while the most bitter and bloody of all times hangs over them like a blossoming almond, and continuous punishments impend like a multitude of flying locusts, and the transgressors are cast out of the way like a black and despicable caper-plant. And the good man shall depart with rejoicing to his own everlasting habitation; but the vile shall fill all their places with wailing, and neither silver laid up in store, nor proved gold, shall be of use anymore. For a mighty stroke shall fall upon all things, even to the pitcher that stands by the well, and the wheel of the vessel which may chance to have been left in the hollow, when the course of time comes to its end and the ablution-bearing period of a life that is like water has passed away. And for men who lie on earth there is but one salvation, that their souls acknowledge and wing their way to Him by whom they have been made. I say, then, again what I have said already, that man's estate is altogether vain, and that nothing can exceed the utter vanity which attaches to the objects of man's inventions. And superfluous is my labor in preaching discreetly, inasmuch as I am attempting to instruct a people here, so indisposed to receive either teaching or healing. And truly the noble man is needed for the understanding of the words of wisdom. Moreover, I, though already aged, and having passed a long life, labored to find out those things which are well-pleasing to God, by means of the mysteries of the truth. And I know that the mind is no less quickened and stimulated by the precepts of the wise, than the body is wont to be when the goad is applied, or a nail is fastened in it. And some will render again those wise lessons which they have received from one good pastor and teacher, as if all with one mouth and in mutual concord set forth in larger detail the truths committed to them. But in many words there is no profit. Neither do I counsel thee, my friend, to write down vain things about what is fitting, from which there in nothing to be gained but weary labor. But, in fine, I shall require to use some such conclusion as this: O men, behold, I charge you now expressly and shortly, that ye fear God, who is at once the Lord and the Overseer of all, and that ye keep also His commandments; and that ye believe that all shall be judged severally in the future, and that every man s receive the just recompense for his deeds, whether they be good or whether they be evil.

Canonical Epistle.

Canon I.

The meats are no burden to us, most holy father, if the captives ate things which their conquerors set before them, especially since there is one report from all, viz., that the barbarians who have made inroads into our parts have not sacrificed to idols. For the apostle says, "Meats for the belly, and the belly for meats: but God shall destroy both it and them." But the Savior also, who cleansed all meats, says, "Not that which goes into a man defiles the man, but that which cometh out." And this meets the case of the captive women defiled by the barbarians, who outraged their bodies. But if the previous life of any such person convicted him of going, as it is written, after the eyes of fornicators, the habit of fornication evidently becomes an object of suspicion also in the time of captivity. And one ought not readily to have communion with such women in prayers. If anyone, however, has lived in the utmost chastity, and has shown in time past a manner of life pure and free from all suspicion, and now falls into wantonness through force of necessity, we have an example for our guidance,—namely, the instance of the damsel in Deuteronomy, whom a man finds in the field, and forces her and lies with her. "Unto the damsel," he says, "ye shall do nothing; there is in the damsel no sin worthy of death: for as when a man rises against his neighbor, and slayed him, even so is this matter: the damsel cried, and there was none to help her."

Canon II.

Covetousness is a great evil; and it is not possible in a single letter to set forth those scriptures in which not robbery alone is declared to be a thing horrible and to be abhorred, but in general the grasping mind, and the disposition to meddle with what belongs to others, in order to satisfy the sordid love of gain. And all persons of that spirit are excommunicated from the Church of God. But that at the time of the irruption, in the midst of such woeful sorrows and bitter lamentations, some should have been audacious enough to consider the crisis which brought destruction to all the very period for their own private aggrandizement, that is a thing which can be averred only of men who are impious and hated of God, and of unsurpassable iniquity. Wherefore it seemed good to excommunicate such persons, lest the wrath (of God) should come upon the whole people, and upon those first of all who are set over them in office, and yet fail to make inquiry. For I am afraid, as the Scripture says, lest the impious work the destruction of the righteous along with his own. "For fornication," it says, "and covetousness *are things* on account of which the wrath of God cometh upon the children of disobedience. Be not ye therefore partakers with them. For ye were sometimes darkness, but now are ye light in the Lord: walk as children of light (for the fruit of the light is in all goodness, and righteousness, and truth), proving what is acceptable unto the Lord. And have no fellowship with the unfruitful works of darkness, but rather reprove them; for it is a shame even to speak of those things which are done of them in secret. But all things that are reproved are made manifest by the light." In this wise speaks the apostle. But if certain parties who pay the proper penalty for that former covetousness of theirs, which exhibited itself in the time of peace, now turn aside again to the indulgence of covetousness in the very time of trouble (i.e., in the troubles of the inroads by the barbarians), and make gain out of the blood and ruin of men who have been utterly despoiled, or taken captive, (or) put to death, what else ought to be expected, than that those who struggle so hotly for covetousness should heap up wrath both for themselves and for the whole people?

Canon III.

Behold, did not Achar the son of Zara transgress in the accursed thing, and trouble then lighted on all the congregation of Israel? And this one man was alone in his sin; but he was not alone in the death that came by his sin. And by us, too, everything of a gainful kind at this time, which is ours not in our own rightful possession, but as property strictly belonging to others, ought to be reckoned a thing devoted. For that Achar indeed took of the spoil; and those men of the present time take also of the spoil. But he took what belonged to enemies; while these now take what belongs to brethren, and aggrandize themselves with fatal gains.

Canon IV.

Let no one deceive himself, nor put forward the pretext of having found such property. For it is not lawful, even for a man who has found anything, to aggrandize himself by it. For Deuteronomy says: "Thou shalt not see thy brother's ox or his sheep go astray in the way, and pay no heed to them; but thou shalt in any wise bring them again unto thy brother. And if thy brother come not nigh thee, or if thou know him not, then thou shalt bring them together, and they shall be with thee until thy brother seek after them, and thou shalt restore them to him again. And in like manner shalt thou do with his ass, and so shalt thou do with his raiment, and so shalt thou do with all lost things of thy brother's, which he hath lost, and thou mayest find." Thus much in Deuteronomy. And in the book of Exodus it is said, with reference not only to the case of finding what is a friend's, but also of finding what is an enemy's: "Thou shalt surely bring them back to the house of their master again." And if it is not lawful to aggrandize oneself at the expense of another, whether he be brother or enemy, even in the time of peace, when he is living at his ease and delicately, and without concern as to his property, how much more must it be the case when one is met by adversity, and is fleeing from his enemies, and has had to abandon his possessions by force of circumstances!

Canon V.

But others deceive themselves by fancying that they can retain the property of others which they may have found as an equivalent for their own property which they have lost. In this way verily, just as the Boradi and Goths brought the havoc of war on them, they make themselves Boradi and Goths to others. Accordingly we have sent to you our brother and comrade in old age, Euphrosynus, with this view, that he may deal with you in accordance with our model here, and teach you against whom you ought to admit accusations, and whom you ought to exclude from your prayers.

Canon VI

Moreover, it has been reported to us that a thing has happened in your country which is surely incredible, and which, if done at all, is altogether the work of unbelievers, and impious men, and men who know not the very name of the Lord; to wit, that some have gone to such a pitch of cruelty and inhumanity, as to be detaining by force certain captives who have made their escape. Dispatch ye commissioners into the country, lest the thunderbolts of heaven fall all too surely upon those who perpetrate such deeds.

Canon VII

Now, as regards those who have been enrolled among the barbarians, and have accompanied them in their irruption in a state of captivity, and who, forgetting that they were from Pontus, and Christians, have become such thorough barbarians, as even to put those of their own race to death by the gibbet or strangulation, and to show their roads or houses to the barbarians, who else would have been ignorant of them, it is necessary for you to debar such persons even from being auditors in the public congregations, until some common decision about them is come to by the saints assembled in council, and by the Holy Spirit antecedently to them.

Canon VIII

Now those who have been so audacious as to invade the houses of others, if they have once been put on their trial and convicted, ought not to be deemed fit even to be hearers in the public congregation. But if they have declared themselves and made restitution, they should be placed in the rank of the repentant.

Canon IX

Now, those who have found in the open field or in their own houses anything left behind them by the barbarians, if they have once been put on their trial and convicted, ought to fall under the same class of the repentant. But if they have declared themselves and made restitution, they ought to be deemed fit for the privilege of prayer.

Canon X.

And they who keep the commandment ought to keep it without any sordid covetousness, demanding neither recompense, nor reward, nor fee, nor anything else that bears the name of acknowledgment.

Canon XI.

Weeping takes place without the gate of the oratory; and the offender standing there ought to implore the faithful as they enter to offer up prayer on his behalf. Waiting on the word, again, takes place within the gate in the porch, where the offender ought to stand until the catechumens *depart*, and thereafter he should go forth. For let him hear the Scriptures and doctrine, it is said, and then be put forth, and reckoned unfit for the privilege of prayer. Submission, again, is that one stands within the gate of the temple, and goes forth along with the catechumens. Restoration is that one be associated with the faithful, and go not forth with the catechumens; and last of all comes the participation in the holy ordinances.

Elucidations.

I.

(The title, p. 18.)

This is a genuine epistle, all but the eleventh canon. It is addressed to an anonymous bishop; one of his suffragans, some think. I suppose, rather, he consults, as Cyprian did, the bishop of the nearest Apostolic See, and awaits his concurrence. It refers to the ravages of the Goths in the days of Gallienus (a.d. 259–267), and proves the care of the Church to maintain discipline, even in times most unfavorable to order and piety. The last canon is an explanatory addition made to elucidate the four degrees or classes of penitents. It is a very interesting document in this respect, and sheds light on the famous canonical epistles of St. Basil.

II.

(Basil the Great, p. 18, note.)

The "Canonical Epistles" of St. Basil are not private letters, but canons of the churches with which he was nearest related. When there was no art of printing, the chief bishops were obliged to communicate with suffragans, and with their brethren in the Apostolic See nearest to them. See them expounded at large in Dupin,

Ecclesiastical Writers of the Fourth Century, Works, vol. i., London, 1693 (translated), p. 139, etc.

III.

(Most holy father, p. 18.)

This expression leads me to think that this epistle is addressed to the Bishop of Antioch or of some other Apostolic See. It must not be taken as a prescribed formula, however, as when we say "Most Reverend" in our days; e.g., addressing the Archbishop of Canterbury. Rather, it is an expression of personal reverence. As yet, titular distinctions, such as these, were not known. In the West existing usages seem to have been introduced with the Carlovingian system of dignities, expounded by Gibbon.

The Oration and Panegyric Addressed to Origen.

Argument I.—For Eight Years Gregory Has Given Up the Practice of Oratory, Being Busied with the Study Chiefly of Roman Law and the Latin Language.

An excellent thing has silence proved itself in many another person on many an occasion, and at present it befits myself, too, most especially, who with or without purpose may keep the door of my lips, and feel constrained to be silent. For I am unpracticed and unskilled in those beautiful and elegant addresses which are spoken or composed in a regular and unbroken train, in select and well-chosen phrases and words; and it may be that I am less apt by nature to cultivate successfully this graceful and truly Grecian art. Besides, it is now eight years since I chanced myself to utter or compose any speech, whether long or short; neither in that period have I heard any other compose or utter anything in private, or deliver in public any laudatory or controversial orations, with the exception of those admirable men who have embraced the noble study of philosophy, and who care less for beauty of language and elegance of expression. For, attaching only a secondary importance to the words, they aim, with all exactness, at investigating and making known the things themselves, precisely as they are severally constituted. Not indeed, in my opinion, that they do not desire, but rather that they do greatly desire, to clothe the noble and accurate results of their thinking in noble and comely language. Yet it may be that they are not able so lightly to put forth this sacred and godlike power (faculty) in the exercise of its own proper conceptions, and at the same time to practice a mode of discourse eloquent in its terms, and thus to comprehend in one and the same mind—and that, too, this little mind of man—two accomplishments, which are the gifts of two distinct persons, and which are, in truth, most contrary to each other. For silence is indeed the friend and helpmeet of thought and invention. But if one aims at readiness of speech and beauty of discourse, he will get at them by no other discipline than the study of words, and their constant practice. Moreover, another branch of learning occupies my mind completely, and the mouth binds the tongue if I should desire to make any speech, however brief, with the voice of the Greeks; I refer to those admirable laws of our sages by which the affairs of all the subjects of the Roman Empire are now directed, and which are neither composed nor learned without difficulty. And these are wise and exact in themselves, and manifold and admirable, and, in a word, most thoroughly Grecian; and they are expressed and committed to us in the Roman tongue, which is a wonderful and magnificent sort of language, and one very aptly conformable to royal authority, but still difficult to me. Nor could it be otherwise with me, even though I might say that it was my desire that it should be. And as our words are nothing else than a kind of imagery of the dispositions of our mind, we should allow those who have the gift of speech, like some good artists alike skilled to the utmost in their art and liberally furnished in the matter of colors, to possess the liberty of painting their word-pictures, not simply of a uniform complexion, but also of various descriptions and of richest beauty in the abundant mixture of flowers, without let or hindrance.

Argument II.—He Essays to Speak of the Well-Nigh Divine Endowments of Origen in His Presence, into Whose Hands He Avows Himself to Have Been Led in a Way Beyond All His Expectation.

But we, like any of the poor, unfurnished with these varied specifics—whether as never having been possessed of them, or, it may be, as having lost them—are under the necessity of using, as it were, only charcoal and tiles, that is to say, those rude and common words and phrases; and by means of these, to the best of our ability, we represent the native dispositions of our mind, expressing them in such language as is at our service, and endeavoring to exhibit the impressions of the figures of our mind, if not clearly or ornately, yet at least with the faithfulness of a charcoal picture, welcoming gladly any graceful and eloquent expression which may present itself from any quarter, although we make little of such. But, furthermore, there is a third circumstance which hinders and dissuades me from this attempt, and which holds me back much more even than the others, and recommends me to keep silence by all means,—I allude to the subject itself, which made me indeed ambitious to speak of it, but which now makes me draw back and delay. For it is my purpose to speak of one who has indeed the semblance and repute of being a man, but who seems, to those who are able to contemplate the greatness of his intellectual caliber, to be endowed with powers nobler and well-nigh divine. And it is not his birth or bodily training that I am about to praise, and that makes me now delay and procrastinate with an excess of caution. Nor, again, is it his strength or beauty; for these form the eulogies of youths, of which it matters little whether the utterance be worthy or not. For, to make an oration on matters of a temporary and fugitive nature, which perish in many various ways and quickly, and to discourse of these with all the grandeur and dignity of great affairs, and with such timorous delays, would seem a vain and futile procedure. And certainly, if it had been proposed to me to speak of any of those things which are useless and unsubstantial, and such as I should never voluntarily have thought of speaking of,—if, I say, it had been proposed to me to speak of anything of that character, my speech would have had none of this caution or fear, lest in any statement I might seem to come beneath the merit of the subject. But now, my subject dealing with that which is most godlike in the man, and that in him which has most affinity with God, that which is indeed confined within the limits of this visible and mortal form, but which strains nevertheless most ardently after the likeness of God; and my object being to make mention of this, and to put my hand to weightier matters, and therein also to express my thanksgivings to the Godhead, in that it has been granted to me to meet with such a man beyond the expectation of men,—the expectation, verily, not only of others, but also of my own heart, for I neither set such a privilege before me at any time, nor hoped for it; it being, I say, my object, insignificant and altogether without understanding as I am, to put my hand to such subjects, it is not without reason that I shrink from the task, and hesitate, and desire to keep silence. And, in truth, to keep silence seems to me to be also the safe course, lest, with the show of an expression of thanksgiving, I may chance, in my rashness, to discourse of noble and sacred subjects in terms ignoble and paltry and utterly trite, and thus not only miss attaining the truth, but even, so far as it depends on me, do it some injury with those who may believe that it stands in such a category, when a discourse which is weak is composed thereon, and is rather calculated to excite ridicule than to prove itself commensurate in its vigor with the dignity of its themes. But all that pertains to thee is beyond the touch of injury and ridicule, O dear soul; or, much rather let me say, that the divine herein remains ever as it is, unmoved and harmed in nothing by our paltry and unworthy words. Yet I know not how we shall escape the imputation of boldness and rashness in thus attempting in our folly, and with little either of intelligence or of preparation, to handle matters which are weighty, and probably beyond our capacity. And if, indeed, elsewhere and with others, we had aspired to make such youthful endeavors in matters like these, we would surely have been bold and daring; nevertheless in such a case our rashness might not have been ascribed to shamelessness, in so far as we should not have been making the bold effort with thee. But now we shall be filling out the whole measure of senselessness, or rather indeed we have already filled it out, in venturing with unwashed feet (as the saying goes) to introduce ourselves to ears into which the Divine Word Himself—not indeed with covered feet, as is the case with the general mass of men, and, as it were, under the thick coverings of enigmatical and obscure sayings, but with unsandalled feet (if one may so speak)—has made His way clearly and perspicuously, and in which He now sojourns; while we, who have but refuse and mud to offer in these human words of ours, have been bold enough to pour them into ears which are practiced in hearing only words that are divine and pure. It might indeed suffice us, therefore, to have transgressed thus far; and now, at least, it might be but right to restrain ourselves, and to advance no further with our discourse. And verily I would stop here most gladly. Nevertheless, as I have once made the rash venture, it may be allowed me first of all to explain the reason under the force of which I have been led into this arduous enterprise, if indeed any pardon can be extended to me for my forwardness in this matter.

Argument III.—He is Stimulated to Speak of Him by the Longing of a Grateful Mind.

To the Utmost of His Ability He Thinks He Ought to Thank Him. From God are the Beginnings of All Blessings; And to Him Adequate Thanks Cannot Be Returned.

Ingratitude appears to me to be a dire evil; a dire evil indeed, yea, the direst of evils. For when one has received some benefit, his failing to attempt to make any return by at least the oral expression of thanks, where aught else is beyond his power, marks him out either as an utterly irrational person, or as one devoid of the sense of obligations conferred, or as a man without any memory. And, again, though one is possessed naturally and at once by the sense and the knowledge of benefits received, yet, unless he also carries the memory of these obligations to future days, and offers some evidence of gratitude to the author of the boons, such a person is a dull, and ungrateful, and impious fellow; and he commits an offense which can be excused neither in the case of the great nor in that of the small:—if we suppose the case of a great and high-minded man not bearing constantly on his lips his great benefits with all gratitude and honor, or that of a small and contemptible man not praising and lauding with all his might one who has been his benefactor, not simply in great services, but also in smaller. Upon the great, therefore, and those who excel in powers of mind, it is incumbent, as out of their greater abundance and larger wealth, to render greater and worthier praise, according to their capacity, to their benefactors. But the humble also, and those in narrow circumstances, it beseems neither to neglect those who do them service, nor to take their services carelessly, nor to flag in heart as if they could offer nothing worthy or perfect; but as poor indeed, and yet as of good feeling, and as measuring not the capacity of him whom they honor, but only their own, they ought to pay him honor according to the present measure of their power,—a tribute which will probably be grateful and pleasant to him who is honored, and in no less consideration with him than it would have been had it been some great and splendid offering, if it is only presented with decided earnestness, and with a sincere mind. Thus is it laid down in the sacred writings, that a certain poor and lowly woman, who was with the rich and powerful that were contributing largely and richly out of their wealth, alone and by herself cast in a small, yea, the very smallest offering, which was, however, all the while her whole substance, and received the testimony of having presented the largest oblation. For, as I judge, the sacred word has not set up the large out- ward quantity of the substance given, but rather the mind and disposition of the giver, as the standard by which the worth and the magnificence of the offering are to be measured. Wherefore it is not meet even for us by any means to shrink from this duty, through the fear that our thanksgivings be not adequate to our obligations; but, on the contrary, we ought to venture and attempt everything, so as to offer thanksgivings, if not adequate, at least such as we have it in our power to exhibit, as in due return. And would that our dis- course, even though it comes short of the perfect measure, might at least reach the mark in some degree, and be saved from all appearance of ingratitude! For a persistent silence, maintained under the plausible cover of an inability to say anything worthy of the subject, is a vain and evil thing; but it is the mark of a good disposition always to make the attempt at a suitable return, even although the power of the person who offers the grateful acknowledgment be inferior to the desert of the subject. For my part, even although I am unable to speak as the matter merits, I shall not keep silence; but when I have done all that I possibly can, then I may congratulate myself. Be this, then, the method of my eucharistic discourse. To God, indeed, the God of the universe, I shall not think of speaking in such terms: yet is it from Him that all the beginnings of our blessings come;

and with Him consequently is it that the beginning of our thanksgivings, or praises, or laudations, ought to be made. But, in truth, not even though I were to devote myself wholly to that duty, and that, too, not as I now am—to wit, profane and impure, and mixed up with and stained by every unhallowed and polluting evil—but sincere and as pure as pure may be, and most genuine, and most unsophisticated, and uncontaminated by anything vile;—not even, I say, though I were thus to devote myself wholly, and with all the purity of the newly born, to this task, should I produce of myself any suitable gift in the way of honor and acknowledgment to the Ruler and Originator of all things, whom neither men separately and individually, nor yet all men in concert, acting with one spirit and one concordant impulse, as though all that is pure were made to meet in one, and all that is diverse from that were turned also to that service, could ever celebrate in a manner worthy of Him. For, in whatsoever measure any man is able to form right and adequate conceptions of His works, and (if such a thing were possible) to speak worthily regarding Him, then, so far as that very capacity is concerned,—a capacity with which he has not been gifted by any other one, but which he has received from Him alone, he cannot possibly find any greater matter of thanksgiving than what is implied in its possession.

Argument IV.—The Son Alone Knows How to Praise the Father Worthily. In Christ and by Christ Our Thanksgivings Ought to Be Rendered to the Father.

Gregory Also Gives Thanks to His Guardian Angel, Because He Was Conducted by Him to Origen.

But let us commit the praises and hymns in honor of the King and Superintendent of all things, the perennial Fount of all blessings, to the hand of Him who, in this matter as in all others, is the Healer of our infirmity, and who alone is able to supply that which is lacking; to the Champion and Savior of our souls, His first-born Word, the Maker and Ruler of all things, with whom also alone it is possible, both for Himself and for all, whether privately and individually, or publicly and collectively, to send up to the Father uninterrupted and ceaseless thanksgivings. For as He is Himself the Truth, and the Wisdom, and the Power of the Father of the universe, and He is besides in Him, and is truly and entirely made one with Him, it cannot be that, either through forgetfulness or unwisdom, or any manner of infirmity, such as marks one dissociated from Him, He shall either fail in the power to praise Him, or, while having the power, shall willingly neglect (a supposition which it is not lawful, surely, to indulge) to praise the Father. For He alone is able most perfectly to fulfil the whole meed of honor which is proper to Him, inasmuch as the Father of all things has made Him one with Himself, and through Him all but completes the circle of His own being objectively, and honors Him with a power in all respects equal to His own, even as also He is honored; which position He first and alone of all creatures that exist has had assigned Him, this Only-begotten of the Father, who is in Him, and who is God the Word; while all others of us are able to express our thanksgiving and our piety only if, in return for all the blessings which proceed to us from the Father, we bring our offerings in simple dependence on Him alone, and thus present the meet oblation of thanksgiving to Him who is the Author of all things, acknowledging also that the only way of piety is in this manner to offer our memorials through Him. Wherefore, in acknowledgment of that ceaseless providence which watches over all of us, alike in the greatest and in the smallest concerns, and which has been sustained even thus far, let this Word be accepted as the worthy and perpetual expression for all thanksgivings and praises,—I mean the altogether perfect and living and verily animate Word of the First Mind Himself. But let this word of ours be taken primarily as an eucharistic address in honor of this sacred personage, who stands alone among all men; and if I may seek to discourse of aught beyond this, and, in particular, of any of those beings who are not seen, but yet are more godlike, and who have a special care for men, it shall be addressed to that being who, by some momentous decision, had me allotted to him from my boyhood to rule, and rear, and train,—I mean that holy angel of God who fed me from my youth, as says the saint dear to God, meaning thereby his own peculiar one. Though he, indeed, as being himself illustrious, did in these terms designate some angel exalted enough to befit his own dignity (and whether it was some other one, or whether it was per- chance the Angel of the Mighty Counsel Himself, the Common Savior of all, that he received as his own peculiar guardian through his perfection, I do not clearly know),—he, I say, did recognize and praise some superior angel as his own, whosoever that was. But we, in addition to the homage we offer to the Common Ruler of all men, acknowledge and praise that being, whosoever he is, who has been the wonderful guide of our childhood, who in all other matters has been in time past my beneficent tutor and guardian. For this office of tutor and guardian is one which evidently can suit neither me nor any of my friends and kindred; for we are all blind, and see nothing of what is before us, so as to be able to judge of what is right and fitting; but it can suit only him who sees beforehand all that is for the good of our soul: *that angel, I say*, who still at this present time sustains, and instructs, and conducts me; and who, in addition to all these other benefits, has brought me into connection with this man, which, in truth, is the most important of all the services done me. And this, too, he has affected for me, although between myself and that man of whom I discourse there was no kinship of race or blood, nor any other tie, nor any relationship in neighborhood or country whatsoever; things which are made the ground of friendship and union among the majority of men. But to speak in brief, in the exercise of a truly divine and wise fore- thought he brought us together, who were unknown to each other, and strangers, and foreigners, separated as thoroughly from each other as intervening nations, and mountains, and rivers can divide man from man, and thus he made good this meeting which has been full of profit to me, having, as I judge, provided beforehand this blessing for me from above from my very birth and earliest upbringing. And in what manner this has been realized it would take long to recount fully, not merely if I were to enter minutely into the whole subject, and were to attempt to omit nothing, but even if, passing many things by, I should purpose simply to mention in a summary way a few of the most important points.

Argument V.—Here Gregory Interweaves the Narrative of His Former Life. His Birth of Heathen Parents is Stated. In the Fourteenth Year of His Age He

Loses His Father. He is Dedicated to the Study of Eloquence and Law. By a Wonderful Leading of Providence, He is Brought to Origen.

For my earliest upbringing from the time of my birth onwards was under the hand of my parents; and the manner of life in my father's house was one of error, and of a kind from which no one, I imagine, expected that we should be delivered; nor had I myself the hope, boy as I was, and without understanding, and under a superstitious father. Then followed the loss of my father, and my orphanhood, which perchance was also the beginning of the knowledge of the truth to me. For then it was that I was brought over first to the word of salvation and truth, in what manner I cannot tell, by constraint rather than by voluntary choice. For what power of decision had I then, who was but fourteen years of age? Yet from this very time this sacred Word began somehow to visit me, just at the period when the reason common to all men attained its full function in me; yea, then for the first time did it visit me. And though I thought but little of this in that olden time, yet now at least, as I ponder it, I consider that no small token of the holy and marvelous providence exercised over me is discernible in this concurrence, which was so distinctly marked in the matter of my years, and which provided that all those deeds of error which preceded that age might be ascribed to youth and want of understanding, and that the Holy Word might not be imparted vainly to a soul yet ungifted with the full power of reason; and which secured at the same time that when the soul now became endowed with that power, though not gifted with the divine and pure reason, it might not be devoid at least of that fear which is accordant with this reason, but that the human and the divine reason might begin to act in me at once and together,—the one giving help with a power to me at least inexplicable, though proper to itself, and the other receiving help. And when I reflect on this, I am filled at once with gladness and with terror, while I rejoice indeed in the leading of providence, and yet am also awed by the fear lest, after being privileged with such blessings, I should still in any way fail of the end. But indeed I know not how my discourse has dwelt so long on this matter, desirous as I am to give an account of the wonderful arrangement (of God's providence) in the course that brought me to this man, and anxious as nevertheless I formerly was to pass with few words to the matters which follow in their order, not certainly imagining that I could render to him who thus dealt with me that tribute of praise, or gratitude, or piety which is due to him (for, were we to designate our discourse in such terms, while yet we said nothing worthy of the theme, we might seem chargeable with arrogance), but simply with the view of offering what may be called a plain narrative or confession, or whatever other humble title may be given it. It seemed good to the only one of my parents who survived to care for me—my mother, namely—that, being already under instruction in those other branches in which boys not ignobly born and nurtured are usually trained, I should attend also a teacher of public speaking, in the hope that I too should become a public speaker. And accordingly I did attend such a teacher; and those who could judge in that department then declared that I should in a short period be a public speaker. I for my own part know not how to pronounce on that, neither should I desire to do so; for there was no apparent ground for that gift then, nor was there as yet any foundation for those forces which were capable of bringing me to it. But that divine conductor and true curator, ever so watchful, when my friends were not thinking of such a step, and when I was not myself desirous of it, came and suggested (an extension of my studies) to one of my teachers under whose charge I had been put, with a view to instruction in the Roman tongue, not in the expectation that I was to reach the completest mastery of that tongue, but only that I might not be absolutely ignorant of it; and this person happened also to be not altogether unversed in laws. Putting the idea, therefore, into this teacher's mind, he set me to learn in a thorough way the laws of the Romans by his help. And that man took up this charge zealously with me; and I, on my side, gave myself to it—more, however, to gratify the man, than as being myself an admirer of the study. And when he got me as his pupil, he began to teach me with all enthusiasm. And he said one thing, which has proved to me the truest of all his sayings, to wit, that my education in the laws would be my greatest *viaticum*—for thus he phrased it—whether I aspired to be one of the public speakers who contend in the courts of justice, or preferred to belong to a different order. Thus did he express himself, intending his word to bear simply on things human; but to me it seems that he was moved to that utterance by a diviner impulse than he himself supposed. For when, willingly or unwillingly, I was becoming well instructed in these laws, at once bonds, as it were, were cast upon my movements, and cause and occasion for my journeying to these parts arose from the city Berytus, which is a city not far distant from this territory, somewhat Latinized, and credited with being a school for these legal studies. And this revered man coming from Egypt, from the city of Alexandria, where previously he happened to have his home, was moved by other circumstances to change his residence to this place, as if with the express object of meeting us. And for my part, I cannot explain the reasons of these incidents, and I shall willingly pass them by. This however is certain, that as yet no necessary occasion for my coming to this place and meeting with this man was afforded by my purpose to learn our laws, since I had it in my power also to repair to the city of Rome itself. How, then, was this affected? The then governor of Palestine suddenly took possession of a friend of mine, namely my sister's husband, and separated him from his wife, and carried him off here against his will, in order to secure his help, and have him associated with him in the labors of the government of the country; for he was a person skilled in law, and perhaps is still so *employed*. After he had gone with him, however, he had the good fortune in no long time to have his wife sent for, and to receive her again, from whom, against his will, and to his grievance, he had been separated. And thus he chanced also to draw us along with her to that same place. For when we were minded to travel, I know not where, but certainly to any other place rather than this, a soldier suddenly came upon the scene, bearing a letter of instructions for us to escort and protect our sister in her restoration to her husband, and to offer ourselves also as companion to her on the journey; in which we had the opportunity of doing a favor to our relative, and most of all to our sister (so that she might not have to address herself to the journey either in any unbecoming manner, or with any great fear or hesitation), while at the same time our other friends and connections thought well of it, and made it out to promise no slight advantage, as we could thus visit the city of Berytus, and carry out there with all diligence our studies in the laws. Thus all things moved me thither,—my sense of duty to my sister, my own studies, and over and above these, the soldier (for it is right also to mention this), who had with him a larger supply of public vehicles than the case demanded, and more cheques than could be required for our sister alone. These were the apparent reasons for our journey; but the secret and yet truer reasons were these,—our opportunity of fellowship with this man, our instruction through that man's means in the truth concerning the Word, and the profit of our soul for its salvation. These were the real causes that brought us here, blind and ignorant, as we were, as to the way of securing our salvation. Wherefore it was not that soldier, but a certain divine companion and beneficent conductor and guardian, ever leading us in safety through the whole of this present life, as through a long journey, that carried us past other places, and Berytus in especial, which city at that time we seemed most bent on reaching, and brought us hither and settled us here, disposing and directing all things, until by any means he might bind us in a connection with this man who was to be the author of the greater part of our blessings. And he who came in such wise, that divine angel, gave over this charge to him, and did, if I may so speak, perchance take his rest here, not indeed under the pressure of labor or exhaustion of any kind (for the generation of those divine ministers knows no weariness), but as having committed us to the hand of a man who would fully discharge the whole work of care and guardianship within his power.

Argument VI.—The Arts by Which Origen Studies to Keep Gregory and His Brother Athenodorus with Him, Although It Was Almost Against Their Will; And the Love by Which Both are Taken Captive. Of Philosophy, the Foundation of Piety, with the View of Giving Himself Therefore Wholly to that Study, Gregory is Willing to Give Up Fatherland, Parents, the Pursuit of Law, and Every Other Discipline. Of the Soul as the Free Principle. The Nobler Part Does Not Desire to Be United with the Inferior, But the Inferior with the Nobler.

And from the very first day of his receiving us (which day was, in truth, the first day to me, and the most precious of all days, if I may so speak, since then for the first time the true Sun began to rise upon me), while we, like some wild creatures of the fields, or like fish, or some sort of birds that had fallen into the toils or nets, and were endeavoring to slip out again and escape, were bent on leaving him, and making off for Berytus or our native country, he studied by all means to associate us closely with him, contriving all kinds of arguments, and putting every rope in motion (as the proverb goes), and bringing all his powers to bear on that object. With that intent he lauded the lovers of philosophy with large laudations and many noble utterances, declaring that those only live a life truly worthy of reason- able creatures who aim at living an upright life and who seek to know first of all themselves, what manner of persons they are, and then the things that are truly good, which man ought to strive after, and then the things that are really evil, from which man ought to flee. And then he reprehended ignorance and all the ignorant: and there are many such, who, like brute cattle, are blind in mind, and have no understanding even of what they are, and are as far astray as though they were wholly void of reason, and neither know themselves what is good and what is evil, nor care at all to learn it from others, but toil feverishly in quest of wealth, and glory, and such honors as belong to the crowd, and bodily comforts, and go distraught about things like these, as if they were the real good. And as though such objects were worth much, yea, worth all else, they prize the things themselves, and the arts by which they can acquire them, and the different lines of life which give scope for their attainment,—the military profession, to wit, and the juridical, and the study of the laws. And with earnest and sagacious words he told us that these are the objects that enervate us, when we despise that reason which ought to be the true master within us. I cannot recount at present all the addresses of this kind which he delivered to us, with the view of persuading us to take up the pursuit of philosophy. Nor was it only for a single day that he thus dealt with us, but for many days and, in fact, as often as we were in the habit of going to him at the outset; and we were pierced by his argumentation as with an arrow from the very first occasion of our hearing him (for he was possessed of a rare combination of a certain sweet grace and persuasiveness, along with a strange power of constraint), though we still wavered and debated the matter undecidedly with ourselves, holding so far by the pursuit of philosophy, without however being brought thoroughly over to it, while somehow or other we found ourselves quite unable to withdraw from it conclusively, and thus were always drawn towards him by the power of his reasonings, as by the force of some superior necessity. For he asserted further that there could be no genuine piety towards the Lord of all in the man who despised this gift of philosophy,—a gift which man alone of all the creatures of the earth has been deemed honorable and worthy enough to possess, and one which every man whatsoever, be he wise or be he ignorant, reasonably embraces, who has not utterly lost the power of thought by some mad distraction of mind. He asserted, then, as I have said, that it was not possible (to speak correctly) for anyone to be truly pious who did not philosophize. And thus he continued to do with us, until, by pouring in upon us many such argumentations, one after the other, he at last carried us fairly off somehow or other by a kind of divine power, like people with his reasonings, and established us (in the practice of philosophy), and set us down without the power of movement, as it were, beside himself by his arts. Moreover, the stimulus of friendship was also brought to bear upon us,—a stimulus, indeed, not easily withstood, but keen and most effective,—the argument of a kind and affectionate disposition, which showed itself benignantly in his words when he spoke to us and associated with us. For he did not aim merely at getting round us by any kind of reasoning; but his desire was, with a benignant, and affectionate, and most benevolent mind, to save us, and make us partakers in the blessings that flow from philosophy, and most especially also in those other gifts which the Deity has bestowed on him above most men, or, as we may perhaps say, above all men of our own time. I mean the power that teaches us piety, the word of salvation, that comes to many, and subdues to itself all whom it visits: for there is nothing that shall resist it, inasmuch as it is and shall be itself the king of all; although as yet it is hidden, and is not recognized, whether with ease or with difficulty, by the common crowd, in such wise that, when interrogated respecting it, they should be able to speak intelligently about it. And thus, like some spark lighting upon our inmost soul, love was kindled and burst into flame within us,—a love at once to the Holy Word, the most lovely object of all, who attracts all irresistibly toward Himself by His unutterable beauty, and to this man, His friend and advocate. And being most mightily smitten by this love, I was persuaded to give up all those objects or pursuits which seem to us befitting, and among others even my boasted jurisprudence,—yea, my very fatherland and friends, both those who were present with me then, and those from whom I had parted. And in my estimation there arose but one object dear and worth desire,—to wit, philosophy, and that master of philosophy, this inspired man. "And the soul of Jonathan was knit with David." This word, indeed, I did not read till afterwards in the sacred Scriptures; but I felt it before that time, not less clearly than it is written: for, in truth, it reached me then by the clearest of all revelations. For it was not simply Jonathan that was knit with David; but those things were knit together which are the ruling powers in man—their souls,—those objects which, even though all the things which are apparent and ostensible in man are severed, cannot by any skill be forced to a severance when they themselves are unwilling. For the soul is free, and cannot be coerced by any means, not even though one should confine it and keep guard over it in some secret prison-house. For wherever the intelligence is, there it is also of its own nature and by the first reason. And if it seems to you to be in a kind of prison-house, it is represented as there to you by a sort of second reason. But for all that, it is by no means precluded from subsisting anywhere according to its own determination; nay, rather it is both able to be, and is reasonably believed to be, there alone and altogether, wheresoever and in connection with what things soever those actions which are proper only to it are in operation. Wherefore, what I experienced has been most clearly declared in this very short statement, that "the soul of Jonathan was knit with the soul of David;" objects which, as I said, cannot by any means be forced to a separation against their will, and which of their own inclination certainly will not readily choose it. Nor is it, in my opinion, in the inferior subject, who is changeful and very prone to vary in purpose, and in whom singly there has been no capacity of union at first, that the power of loosing the sacred bonds of this affection rests, but rather in the nobler one, who is constant and not readily shaken, and through whom it has been possible to tie these bonds and to fasten this sacred knot. Therefore it is not the soul of David that was knit by the divine word with the soul of Jonathan; but, on the contrary, the soul of the latter, who was the inferior, is said to be thus affected and knit with the soul of David. For the nobler object would not choose to be knit with one inferior, inasmuch as it is sufficient for itself; but the inferior object, as standing in need of the help which the nobler can give, ought properly to be knit with the nobler, and fitted dependently to it: so that this latter, retaining still its sufficiency in itself, might sustain no loss by its connection with the inferior; and that that which is of itself without order being now united and fitted harmoniously with the nobler, might, without any detriment done, be perfectly subdued to the nobler by the constraints of such bonds. Wherefore, to apply the bonds is the part of the superior, and not of the inferior; but to be knit to the other is the part of the inferior, and this too in such a manner that it shall possess no power of loosing itself from these bonds. And by a similar constraint, then, did this David of ours once gird us to himself; and he holds us now, and has held us ever since that time, so that, even though we desired it, we could not loose ourselves from his bonds. And hence it follows that, even though we were to depart, he would not release this soul of mine, which, as the Holy Scripture puts it, he holds knit so closely with himself.

Argument VII.—The Wonderful Skill with Which Origen Prepares Gregory and Athenodorus for Philosophy. The Intellect of Each is Exercised First in Logic, and the Mere Attention to Words is Contemned.

But after he had thus carried us captive at the very outset, and had shut us in, as it were, on all sides, and when what was best had been accomplished by him, and when it seemed good to us to remain with him for a time, then he took us in hand, as a skilled husbandman may take in hand some field unwrought, and altogether unfertile, and sour, and burnt up, and hard as a rock, and rough, or, it may be, one not utterly barren or unproductive, but rather, perchance, by nature very productive, though then waste and neglected, and stiff and intractable with thorns and wild shrubs; or as a gardener may take in hand some plant which is wild indeed, and which yields no cultivated fruits, though it may not be absolutely worthless, and on finding it thus, may, by his skill in gardening, bring some cultivated shoot and graft it in, by making a fissure in the middle, and then bringing the two together, and binding the one to the other, until the sap in each shall flow in one stream, and they shall both grow with the same nurture: for one may often see a tree of a mixed and worthless species thus rendered productive in spite of its past barrenness, and made to rear the fruits of the good olive on wild roots; or one may see a wild plant saved from being altogether profitless by the skill of a careful gardener; or, once more, one may see a plant which other- wise is one both of culture and of fruitfulness, but which, through the want of skilled attendance, has been left unpruned and unwatered and waste, and which is thus choked by the mass of superfluous shoots suffered to grow out of it at random, yet brought to discharge its proper function in germination, and made to bear the fruit whose production was formerly hindered by the superfluous growth. In such wise, then, and with such a disposition did he receive us at first; and surveying us, as it were, with a husbandman's skill, and gauging us thoroughly, and not confining his notice to those things only which are patent to the eye of all, and which are looked upon in open light, but penetrating into us more deeply, and probing what is most inward in us, he put us to the question, and made propositions to us, and listened to us in our replies; and whenever he thereby detected anything in us not wholly fruitless and profitless and waste, he set about clearing the soil, and turning it up and irrigating it, and putting all things in movement, and brought his whole skill and care to bear on us, and wrought upon our mind. And thorns and thistles, of wild herb or plant which our mind (so unregulated and precipitate in its own action) yielded and produced in its uncultured luxuriance and native wildness, he cut out and thoroughly removed by the processes of refutation and prohibition; sometimes assailing us in the genuine Socratic fashion, and again upsetting us by his argumentation whenever he saw us getting restive under him, like so many unbroken steeds, and springing out of the course and galloping madly about at random, until with a strange kind of persuasiveness and constraint he reduced us to a state of quietude under him by his discourse, which acted like a bridle in our mouth. And that was at first an unpleasant position for us, and one not without pain, as he dealt with people who were unused to it, and still all untrained to submit to reason, when he plied us with his argumentations; and yet he purged us by them. And when he had made us adaptable, and had prepared us successfully for the reception of the words of truth, then, further, as though we were now a soil well-wrought and soft, and ready to impart growth to the seeds cast into it, he dealt liberally with us, and sowed the good seed in season, and attended to all the other cares of the good husbandry, each in its own proper season. And whenever he perceived any element of infirmity or baseness in our mind (whether it was of that character by nature, or had become thus gross through the excessive nurture of the body), he pricked it with his discourses, and reduced it by those delicate words and turns of reasoning which, although at first the very simplest, are gradually evolved one after the other, and skillfully wrought out, until they advance to a sort of complexity which can scarce be mastered or unfolded, and which cause us to start up, as it were, out of sleep, and teach us the art of holding always by what is immediately before one, without ever making any slip by reason either of length or of subtlety. And if there was in us anything of an injudicious and precipitate tendency, whether in the way of assenting to all that came across us, of whatever character the objects might be, and even though they proved false, or in the way of often withstanding other things, even though they were spoken truth- fully,— that, too, he brought under discipline in us by those delicate reasonings already mentioned, and by others of like kind (for this branch of philosophy is of varied form), and accustomed us not to throw in our testimony at one time, and again to refuse it, just at random, and as chance impelled, but to give it only after careful examination not only into things manifest, but also into those that are secret. For many things which are in high repute of themselves, and honorable in appearance, have found entrance through fair words into our ears, as though they were true, while yet they were hollow and false, and have borne off and taken possession of the suffrage of truth at our hand, and then, no long time afterwards, they have been discovered to be corrupt and unworthy of credit, and deceitful borrowers of the garb of truth; and have thus too easily exposed us as men who are ridiculously deluded, and who bear their witness inconsiderately to things which ought by no means to have won it. And, on the contrary, other things which are really honorable and the reverse of impositions, but which have not been expressed in plausible statements, and thus have the appearance of being paradoxical and most incredible, and which have been rejected as false on their own showing, and held up undeservedly to ridicule, have afterwards, on careful investigation and examination, been discovered to be the truest of all things, and wholly incontestable, though for a time spurned and reckoned false. Not simply, then, by dealing with things patent and prominent, which are sometimes delusive and sophistical, but also by teaching us to search into things within us, and to put them all individually to the test, lest any of them should give back a hollow sound, and by instructing us to make sure of these inward things first of all, he trained us to give our assent to outward things only then and thus, and to express our opinion on all these severally. In this way, that capacity of our mind which deals critically with words and reasonings, was educated in a rational manner; not according to the judgments of illustrious rhetoricians—whatever Greek or foreign honor appertains to that title—for theirs is a discipline of little value and no necessity: but in accordance with that which is most needful for all, whether Greek or outlandish, whether wise or illiterate, and, in fine, not to make a long statement by going over every profession and pursuit separately, in accordance with that which is most indispensable for all men, whatever manner of life they have chosen, if it is indeed the care and interest of all who have to converse on any subject whatever with each other, to be protected against deception.

Argument VIII.—Then in Due Succession He Instructs Them in Physics, Geometry, and Astronomy.

Nor did he confine his efforts merely to that form of the mind which it is the lot of the dialectics to regulate; but he also took in hand that humble capacity of mind, (which shows itself) in our amazement at the magnitude, and the wondrousness, and the magnificent and absolutely wise construction of the world, and in our marveling in a reasonless way, and in our being overpowered with fear, and in our knowing not, like the irrational creatures, what conclusion to come to. That, too, he aroused and corrected by other studies in natural science, illustrating and distinguishing the various divisions of created objects, and with admirable clearness reducing them to their pristine elements, taking them all up perspicuously in his discourse, and going over the nature of the whole, and of each several section, and discussing the multiform revolution and mutation of things in the world, until he carried us fully along with him under his clear teaching; and by those reasonings which he had partly learned from others, and partly found out for himself, he filled our minds with a rational instead of an irrational wonder at the sacred economy of the universe, and irreproveable constitution of all things. This is that sublime and heavenly study which is taught by natural philosophy—a science most attractive to all. And what need is there now to speak of the sacred mathematics, viz., geometry, so precious to all and above all controversy, and astronomy, whose course is on high? These different studies he imprinted on our understandings, training us in them, or calling them into our mind, or doing with us something else which I know not how to designate rightly. And the one he presented lucidly as the immutable groundwork and secure foundation of all, namely geometry; and by the other, namely astronomy, he lifted us up to the things that are highest above us, while he made heaven passable to us by the help of each of these sciences, as though they were ladders reaching the skies.

Argument IX.—But He Imbues Their Minds, Above All, with Ethical Science; And He Does Not Confine Himself to Discoursing on the Virtues in Word, But He Rather Confirms His Teaching by His Acts.

Moreover, as to those things which excel all in importance, and those for the sake of which, above all else, the whole family of the philosophical labors, gathering them like good fruits produced by the varied growths of all the other studies, and of long practiced philosophizing,—I mean the divine virtues that concern the moral nature, by which the impulses of the mind have their equable and stable subsistence,—through these, too, he aimed at making us truly proof against grief and disquietude under the pressure of all ills, and at imparting to us a well-disciplined and steadfast and religious spirit, so that we might be in all things veritably blessed. And this he toiled at effecting by pertinent discourses, of a wise and soothing tendency, and very often also by the most cogent addresses touching our moral dispositions, and our modes of life. Nor was it only by words, but also by deeds, that he regulated in some measure our inclinations,—to wit, by that very contemplation and observation of the impulses and affections of the mind, by the issue of which most especially the mind is wont to be reduced to a right estate from one of discord, and to be re- stored to a condition of judgment and order out of one of confusion. So that, beholding itself as in a mirror (and I may say specifically, viewing, on the one hand, the very beginnings and roots of evil in it, and all that is reasonless within it, from which spring up all absurd affections and passions; and, on the other hand, all that is truly excellent and reasonable within it, under the sway of which it remains proof against injury and perturbation in itself and then scrutinizing carefully the things thus discovered to be in it), it might cast out all those which are the growth of the inferior part, and which waste our powers through intemperance, or hinder and choke them through depression,—such things as pleasures and lusts, or pains and fears, and the whole array of ills that accompany these different species of evil. I say that thus it might cast them out and make away with them, by coping with them while yet in their beginnings and only just commencing their growth, and not leaving them to wax in strength even by a short delay, but destroying and rooting them out at once; while, at the same time, it might foster all those things which are really good, and which spring from the nobler part, and might preserve them by nursing them in their beginnings, and watching carefully over them until they should reach their maturity. For it is thus (he used to say) that the heavenly virtues will ripen in the soul: to wit, prudence, which first of all is able to judge of those very motions in the mind at once from the things themselves, and by the knowledge which accrues to it of things outside of us, whatever such there maybe, both good and evil; and temperance, the power that makes the right selection among these things in their beginnings; and righteousness, which assigns what is just to each; and that virtue which is the conserver of them all—fortitude. And therefore he did not accustom us to a mere profession in words, as that prudence, for instance, is the knowledge of good and evil, or of what ought to be done, and what ought not: for that would be indeed a vain and profitless study, if there was simply the doctrine without the deed; and worthless would that prudence be, which, without doing the things that ought to be done, and without turning men away from those that ought not to be done, should be able merely to furnish the knowledge of these things to those who possessed her,—though many such persons come under our observation. Nor, again, did he content himself with the mere assertion that temperance is simply the knowledge of what ought to be chosen and what ought not; though the other schools of philosophers do not teach even so much as that, and especially the more recent, who are so forcible and vigorous in words (so that I have often been astonished at them, when they sought to demonstrate that there is the same virtue in God and in men, and that upon earth, in particular, the wise man is equal to God), and yet are incapable of delivering the truth as to prudence, so that one shall do the things which are dictated by prudence, or the truth as to temperance, so that one shall choose the things he has learned by it; and the same holds good also of their treatment of righteousness and fortitude. Not thus, however, in mere words only did this teacher go over the truths concerning the virtues with us; but he incited us much more to the practice of virtue, and stimulated us by the deeds he did more than by the doctrines he taught.

Argument X.—Hence the Mere Word-Sages are Confuted, Who Say and Yet Act Not.

Now I beg of the philosophers of this present time, both those whom I have known personally myself, and those of whom I have heard by report from others, and I beg also of all other men, that they take in good part the statements I have just made. And let no one suppose that I have expressed myself thus, either through simple friendship toward that man, or through hatred toward the rest of the philosophers; for if there is any one inclined to be an admirer of them for their discourses, and wishful to speak well of them, and pleased at hearing the most honorable mention made of them by others, I myself am the man. Nevertheless, those facts (to which I have referred) are of such a nature as to bring upon the very name of philosophy the last degree of ridicule almost from the great mass of men; and I might almost say that I would choose to be altogether unversed in it, rather than learn any of the things which these men profess, with whom I thought it good no longer to associate myself in this life,—though in that, it may be, I formed an incorrect judgment. But I say that no one should suppose that I make these statements at the mere prompting of a zealous regard for the praise of this man, or under the stimulus of any existing animosity towards other philosophers. But let all be assured that I say even less than his deeds merit, lest I should seem to be indulging in adulation; and that I do not seek out studied words and phrases, and cunning means of laudation—I who could never of my own will, even when I was a youth, and learning the popular style of address under a professor of the art of public speaking, bear to utter a word of praise, or pass any encomium on any one which was not genuine. Wherefore on the present occasion, too, I do not think it right in proposing to myself the task simply of commending him, to magnify him at the cost of the reprobation of others. And, in good sooth, I should speak only to the man's injury, if, with the view of having something grander to say of him, I should compare his blessed life with the failings of others. We are not, however, so senseless. But I shall testify simply to what has come within my own experience, apart from all ill-judged comparisons and trickeries in words.

Argument XI.—Origen is the First and the Only One that Exhorts Gregory to Add to

His Acquirements the Study of Philosophy, and Offers Him in a Certain Manner an Example in Himself. Of Justice, Prudence, Temperance, and Fortitude. The Maxim, Know Thyself. He was also the first and only man that urged me to study the philosophy of the Greeks, and persuaded me by his own moral example both to hear and to hold by the doctrine of morals, while as yet I had by no means been won over to that, so far as other philosophers were concerned (I again acknowledge it),—not rightly so, indeed, but unhappily, as I may say without exaggeration, for me. I did not, however, associate with many at first, but only with some few who professed to be teachers, though, in good sooth, they all established their philosophy only so far as words went. This man, however, was the first that induced me to philosophize by his words, as he pointed the exhortation by deeds before he gave it in words, and did not merely recite well-studied sentences; nay, he did not deem it right to speak on the subject at all, but with a sincere mind, and one bent on striving ardently after the practical accomplishment of the things expressed, and he endeavored all the while to show himself in character like the man whom he describes in his discourses as the person who shall lead a noble life, and he ever exhibited (in himself), I would say, the pattern of the wise man. But as our discourse at the outset proposed to deal with the truth, and not with vainglorious language, I shall not speak of him now as the exemplar of the wise man. And yet, if I chose to speak thus of him, I should not be far astray from the truth. Nevertheless, I pass that by at present. I shall not speak of him as a perfect pattern, but as one who vehemently desires to imitate the perfect pattern, and strives after it with zeal and earnestness, even beyond the capacity of men, if I may so express myself; and who labors, moreover, also to make us, who are so different, of like character with himself, not mere masters and apprehenders of the bald doctrines concerning the impulses of the soul, but masters and apprehenders of these impulses themselves. For he pressed us on both to deed and to doctrine, and carried us along by that same view and method, not merely into a small section of each virtue, but rather into the whole, if mayhap we were able to take it in. And he constrained us also, if I may so speak, to practice righteousness on the ground of the personal action of the soul itself, which he persuaded us to study, drawing us off from the officious anxieties of life, and from the turbulence of the forum, and raising us to the nobler vocation of looking into ourselves, and dealing with the things that concern ourselves in truth. Now, that this is to practice righteousness, and that this is the true righteousness, some also of our ancient philosophers have asserted (expressing it as the *personal action*, I think), and have affirmed that this is more profitable for blessedness, both to the men themselves and to those who are with them, if indeed it belongs to this virtue to recompense according to desert, and to assign to each his own. For what else could be supposed to be so proper to the soul? Or what could be so worthy of it, as to exercise a care over itself, not gazing outwards, or busying itself with alien matters, or, to speak shortly, doing the worst injustice to itself, but turning its attention inwardly upon itself, rendering its own due to itself, and acting thereby righteously? To practice righteousness after this fashion, therefore, he impressed upon us, if I may so speak, by a sort of force. And he educated us to prudence none the less,—teaching to be at home with ourselves, and to desire and endeavor to know ourselves, which indeed is the most excellent achievement of philosophy, the thing that is ascribed also to the most prophetic of spirits as the highest argument of wisdom—the precept, *Know thyself*. And that this is the genuine function of prudence, and that such is the heavenly prudence, is affirmed well by the ancients; for in this there is one virtue common to God and to man; while the soul is exercised in beholding itself as in a mirror, and reflects the divine mind in itself, if it is worthy of such a relation, and traces out a certain inexpressible method for the attaining of a kind of apotheosis. And in correspondence with this come also the virtues of temperance and fortitude: temperance, indeed, in conserving this very prudence which must be in the soul that knows itself, if that is ever its lot (for this temperance, again, surely means just a sound prudence): and fortitude, in keeping steadfastly by all the duties which have been spoken of, without falling away from them, either voluntarily or under any force, and in keeping and holding by all that has been laid down. For he teaches that this virtue acts also as a kind of preserver, maintainer, and guardian.

Argument XII.—Gregory Disallows Any Attainment of the Virtues on His Part. Piety is Both the Beginning and the End, and Thus It is the Parent of All the Virtues.

It is true, indeed that in consequence of our dull and sluggish nature, he has not yet succeeded in making us righteous, and prudent, and temperate, or manly, although he has labored zealously on us. For we are neither in real possession of any virtue whatsoever, either human or divine, nor have we ever made any near approach to it, but we are still far from it. And these are very great and lofty virtues, and none of them may be assumed by any common person, but only by one whom God inspires with the power. We are also by no means so favorably constituted for them by nature, neither do we yet profess ourselves to be worthy of reaching them; for through our listlessness and feebleness we have not done all these things which ought to be done by those who aspire after what is noblest, and aim at what is perfect. We are not yet therefore either righteous or temperate, or endowed with any of the other virtues. But this admirable man, this friend and advocate of the virtues, has long ago done for us perhaps all that it lay in his power to do for us, in making us lovers of virtue, who should love it with the most ardent affection. And by his own virtue he created in us a love at once for the beauty of righteousness, the golden face of which in truth was shown to us by him; and for prudence, which is worthy of being sought by all; and for the true wisdom, which is most delectable; and for temperance, the heavenly virtue which forms the sound constitution of the soul, and brings peace to all who possess it; and for manliness, that most admirable grace; and for patience, that virtue peculiarly ours; and, above all, for piety, which men rightly designate when they call it the mother of the virtues. For this is the beginning and the end of all the virtues. And beginning with this one, we shall find all the other virtues grow upon us most readily: if, while for ourselves we earnestly aspire after this grace, which every man, be he only not absolutely impious, or a mere pleasure- seeker, ought to acquire for himself, in order to his being a friend of God and a maintainer of His truth, and while we diligently pursue this virtue, we also give heed to the other virtues, in order that we may not approach our God in unworthiness and impurity, but with all virtue and wisdom as our best conductors and most sagacious priests. And the end of all I consider to be nothing but this: By the pure mind make thyself like to God, that thou mayest draw near to Him, and abide in Him.

Argument XIII.—The Method Which Origen Used in His Theological and Metaphysical Instructions. He

Commends the Study of All Writers, the Atheistic Alone Excepted. The Marvelous Power of Persuasion in Speech. The Facility of the Mind in Giving Its Assent.

And besides all his other patient and laborious efforts, how shall I in words give any account of what he did for us, in instructing us in theology and the devout character? and how shall I enter into the real disposition of the man, and show with what judiciousness and careful preparation he would have us familiarized with all discourse about the Divinity, guarding sedulously against our being in any peril with respect to what is the most needful thing of all, namely, the knowledge of the Cause of all things? For he deemed it right for us to study philosophy in such wise, that we should read with utmost diligence all that has been written, both by the philosophers and by the poets of old, rejecting nothing, and repudiating nothing (for, indeed, we did not yet possess the power of critical discernment), except only the productions of the atheists, who, in their conceits, lapse from the general intelligence of man, and deny that there is either a God or a providence. From these he would have us abstain, because they are not worthy of being read, and because it might chance that the soul within us that is meant for piety might be defiled by listening to words that are contrary to the worship of God. For even those who frequent the temples of piety, as they think them to be, are careful not to touch anything that is profane. He held, therefore, that the books of such men did not merit to be taken at all into the consideration of men who have assumed the practice of piety. He thought, however, that we should obtain and make ourselves familiar with all other writings, neither preferring nor repudiating any one kind, whether it be philosophical discourse or not, whether

Greek or foreign, but hearing what all of them have to convey. And it was with great wisdom and sagacity that he acted on this principle, lest any single saying given by the one class or the other should be heard and valued above others as alone true, even though it might not be true, and lest it might thus enter our mind and deceive us, and, in being lodged there by itself alone, might make us its own, so that we should no more have the power to withdraw from it, or wash ourselves clear of it, as one washes out a little wool that has got some color ingrained in it. For a mighty thing and an energetic is the discourse of man, and subtle with its sophisms, and quick to find its way into the ears, and mold the mind, and impress us with what it conveys; and when once it has taken possession of us, it can win us over to love it as truth; and it holds its place within us even though it be false and deceitful, overmastering us like some enchanter, and retaining as its champion the very man it has deluded. And, on the other hand, the mind of man is withal a thing easily deceived by speech, and very facile in yielding its assent; and, indeed, before it discriminates and inquiries into matters in any proper way, it is easily won over, either through its own obtuseness and imbecility, or through the subtlety of the discourse, to give itself up, at random often, all weary of accurate examination, to crafty reasonings and judgments, which are erroneous themselves, and which lead into error those who receive them. And not only so; but if another mode of discourse aims at correcting it, it will neither give it admittance, nor suffer itself to be altered in opinion, because it is held fast by any notion which has previously got possession of it, as though some inexorable tyrant were lording over it.

Argument XIV.—Whence the Contentions of Philosophers Have Sprung. Against Those Who Catch at Everything that Meets Them, and Give It Credence, and Cling to It. Origen Was in the Habit of Carefully Reading and Explaining the Books of the Heathen to His Disciples.

Is it not thus that contradictory and opposing tenets have been introduced, and all the contentions of philosophers, while one party withstands the opinions of another, and some hold by certain positions, and others by others, and one school attaches itself to one set of dogmas, and another to another? And all, indeed, aim at philosophizing, and profess to have been doing so ever since they were first roused to it, and declare that they desire it not less now when they are well versed in the discussions than when they began them: yea, rather they allege that they have even more love for philosophy now, after they have had, so to speak, a little taste of it, and have had the liberty of dwelling on its discussions, than when at first, and without any previous experience of it, they were urged by a sort of impulse to philosophize. That is what they say; and henceforth they give no heed to any words of those who hold opposite opinions. And accordingly, no one of the ancients has ever induced any one of the moderns, or those of the Peripatetic school, to turn to his way of thinking, and adopt his method of philosophizing; and, on the other hand, none of the moderns has imposed his notions upon those of the ancient school. Nor, in short, has anyone done so with any other. For it is not an easy thing to induce one to give up his own opinions, and accept those of others; although these might, perhaps, even be sentiments which, if he had been led to credit them before he began to philosophize, the man might at first have admired and accepted with all readiness: as, while the mind was not yet preoccupied, he might have directed his attention to that set of opinions, and given them his approval, and on their behalf opposed himself to those which he holds at present. Such, at least, has been the kind of philosophizing exhibited by our noble and most eloquent and critical Greeks: for whatever any one of these has lighted on at the outset, moved by some impulse or other, that alone he declares to be truth, and holds that all else which is maintained by other philosophers is simply delusion and folly, though he himself does not more satisfactorily establish his own positions by argument, than do all the others severally defend their peculiar tenets; the man's object being simply to be under no obligation to give up and alter his opinions, whether by constraint or by persuasion, while he has (if one may speak truth) nothing else but a kind of unreasoning impulse towards these dogmas on the side of philosophy, and possesses no other criterion of what he imagines to be true, than (let it not seem an incredible assertion) undistinguishing chance. And as each one thus becomes attached to those positions with which he has first fallen in, and is, as it were, held in chains by them, he is no longer capable of giving attention to others, if he happens to have anything of his own to offer on every subject with the demonstration of truth, and if he has the aid of argument to show how false the tenets of his adversaries are; for, helplessly and thoughtlessly and as if he looked for some happy contingency, he yields himself to the reasonings that first take possession of him. And such reasonings mislead those who accept them, not only in other matters, but above all, in what is of greatest and most essential consequence—in the knowledge of God and in piety. And yet men become bound by them in such a manner that no one can very easily release them. For they are like men caught in a swamp stretching over some wide impassable plain, which, when they have once fallen into it, allows them neither to retrace their steps nor to cross it and effect their safety, but keeps them down in its soil until they meet their end; or they may be compared to men in a deep, dense, and majestic forest, into which the wayfarer enters, with the idea, perchance, of finding his road out of it again forthwith, and of taking his course once more on the open plain, but is baffled in his purpose by the extent and thickness of the wood. And turning in a variety of directions, and lighting on various continuous paths within it, he pursues many a course, thinking that by some of them he will surely find his way out: but they only lead him farther in, and in no way open up an exit for him, inasmuch as they are all only paths within the forest itself; until at last the traveler, utterly worn out and exhausted, seeing that all the ways he had tried had proved only forest still, and despairing of finding any more his dwelling-place on earth, makes up his mind to abide there, and establish his hearth, and lay out for his use such free space as he can prepare in the wood itself. Or again, we might take the similitude of a labyrinth, which has but one apparent entrance, so that one suspects nothing artful from the outside, and goes within by the single door that shows itself; and then, after advancing to the farthest interior, and viewing the cunning spectacle, and examining the construction so skillfully contrived, and full of passages, and laid out with unending paths leading inwards or outwards, he decides to go out again, but finds himself unable, and sees his exit completely intercepted by that inner construction which appeared such a triumph of cleverness. But, after all, there is neither any labyrinth so inextricable and intricate, nor any forest so dense and devious, nor any plain or swamp so difficult for those to get out of, who have once got within it, as is discussion, at least as one may meet with it in the case of certain of these philosophers. Wherefore, to secure us against falling into the unhappy experience of most, he did not introduce us to any one exclusive school of philosophy; nor did he judge it proper for us to go away with any single class of philosophical opinions, but he introduced us to all, and determined that we should be ignorant of no kind of Grecian doctrine. And he himself went on with us, preparing the way before us, and leading us by the hand, as on a journey, whenever anything tortuous and unsound and delusive came in our way. And he helped us like a skilled expert who has had long familiarity with such subjects, and is not strange or inexperienced in anything of the kind, and who therefore may remain safe in his own altitude, while he stretches forth his hand to others, and effects their security too, as one drawing up the submerged. Thus did he deal with us, selecting and setting before us all that was useful and true in all the various philosophers, and putting aside all that was false. And this he did for us, both in other branches of man's knowledge, and most especially in all that concerns piety.

Argument XV.—The Case of Divine Matters. Only God and His Prophets are to Be Heard in These. The Prophets and Their Auditors are Acted on by the Same Afflatus. Origen's Excellence in the Interpretation of Scripture.

With respect to these human teachers, indeed, he counselled us to attach ourselves to none of them, not even though they were attested as most wise by all men, but to devote ourselves to God alone, and to the prophets. And he himself became the interpreter of the prophets to us, and explained whatsoever was dark or enigmatical in them. For there are many things of that kind in the sacred words; and whether it be that God is pleased to hold communication with men in such a way as that the divine word may not enter all naked and uncovered into an unworthy soul, such as many are, or whether it be, that while every divine oracle is in its own nature most clear and perspicuous, it seems obscure and dark to us, who have apostatized from God, and have lost the faculty of hearing through time and age, I cannot tell. But however the case may stand, if it be that there are some words really enigmatical, he explained all such, and set them in the light, as being himself a skilled and most discerning hearer of God; or if it be that none of them are really obscure in their own nature, they were also not unintelligible to him, who alone of all men of the present time with whom I have myself been acquainted, or of whom I have heard by the report of others, has so deeply studied the clear and luminous oracles of God, as to be able at once to receive their meaning into his own mind, and to convey it to others. For that Leader of all men, who inspires God's dear prophets, and suggests all their prophecies and their mystic and heavenly words, has honored this man as He would a friend, and has constituted him an expositor of these same oracles; and things of which He only gave a hint by others, He made matters of full instruction by this man's instrumentality; and in things which He, who is worthy of all trust, either enjoined in regal fashion, or simply enunciated, He imparted to this man the gift of investigating and unfolding and explaining them: so that, if there chanced to be any one of obtuse and incredulous mind, or one again thirsting for instruction, he might learn from this man, and in some manner be constrained to understand and to decide for belief, and to follow God. These things, moreover, as I judge, he gives forth only and truly by participation in the Divine Spirit: for there is need of the same power for those who prophesy and for those who hear the prophets; and no one can rightly hear a prophet, unless the same Spirit who prophesies bestows on him the capacity of apprehending His words. And this principle is expressed indeed in the Holy Scriptures themselves, when it is said that only He who shutted opened, and no other one whatever: and what is shut is opened when the word of inspiration explains mysteries. Now that greatest gift this man has received from God, and that noblest of all endowments he has had bestowed upon him from heaven, that he should be an interpreter of the oracles of God to men, and that he might understand the words of God, even as if God spoke them to him, and that he might recount them to men in such wise as that they may hear them with intelligence. Therefore to us there was no forbidden subject of speech; for there was no matter of knowledge hidden or in- accessible to us, but we had it in our power to learn every kind of discourse, both foreign and Greek, both spiritual and political, both divine and human; and we were permitted with all freedom to go round the whole circle of knowledge, and investigate it, and satisfy ourselves with all kinds of doctrines, and enjoy the sweets of intellect. And whether it was some ancient system of truth, or whether it was something one might otherwise name that was before us, we had in him an apparatus and a power at once admirable and full of the most beautiful views. And to speak in brief, he was truly a paradise to us after the similitude of the paradise of God, wherein we were not set indeed to till the soil beneath us, or to make ourselves gross with bodily nurture, but only to increase the acquisitions of mind with all gladness and enjoyment,—planting, so to speak, some fair growths ourselves, or having them planted in us by the Author of all things.

Argument XVI.—Gregory Laments His Departure Under a Threefold Comparison; Likening It to Adam's Departure Out of Paradise. To the Prodigal Son's Abandonment of His Father's House, and to the Deportation of the Jews into Babylon.

Here, truly, is the paradise of comfort; here are true gladness and pleasure, as we have enjoyed them during this period which is now at its end—no short space indeed in itself, and yet all too short if this is really to be its conclusion, when we depart and leave this place behind us. For I know not what has possessed me, or what offence has been committed by me, that I should now be going away—that I should now be put away. I know not what I should say, unless it be that I am like a second Adam and have begun to talk, outside of paradise. How excellent might my life be, were I but a listener to the addresses of my teacher, and silent myself! Would that even now I could have learned to be mute and speechless, rather than to present this new spectacle of making the teacher the hearer! For what concern had I with such a harangue as this? and what obligation was there upon me to make such an address, when it became me not to depart, but to cleave fast to the place? But these things seem like the transgressions that sprung from the pristine deceit, and the penalties of these primeval offences still await me here. Do I not appear to myself to be dis- obedient in daring thus to overpass the words of God, when I ought to abide in them, and hold by them? And in that I withdraw, I flee from this blessed life, even as the primeval man fled from the face of God, and I return to the soil from which I was taken. Therefore shall I have to eat of the soil all the days of my life there, and I shall have to till the soil—the very soil which produces thorns and thistles for me, that is to say, pains and reproachful anxieties—set loose as I shall be from cares that are good and noble. And what I left behind me before, to that I now return—to the soil, as it were, from which I came, and to my common relationships here below, and to my father's house—leaving the good soil, where of old I knew not that the good fatherland lay; leaving also the relations in whom at a later period I began to recognize the true kinsmen of my soul, and the house, too, of him who is in truth our father, in which the father abides, and is piously honored and revered by the genuine sons, whose desire it also is to abide therein. But I, destitute alike of all piety and worthiness, am going forth from the number of these, and am turning back to what is behind, and am retracing my steps. It is recorded that a certain son, receiving from his father the portion of goods that fell to him proportionately with the other heir, his brother, departed, by his own determination, into a strange country far distant from his father; and, living there in riot, he scattered his ancestral substance, and utterly wasted it; and at last, under the pressure of want, he hired himself as a swine-herd; and being driven to extremity by hunger, he longed to share the food given to the swine, but could not touch it. Thus did he pay the penalty of his dissolute life, when he had to exchange his father's table, which was a princely one, for something he had not looked forward to—the sustenance of swine and serfs. And we also seem to have some such fortune before us, now that we are departing, and that, too, without the full portion that falls to us. For though we have not received all that we ought, we are nevertheless going away, leaving behind us what is noble and dear with you and beside you, and taking in exchange only what is inferior. For all things melancholy will now meet us in succession,—tumult and confusion instead of peace, and an un- regulated life instead of one of tranquility and harmony, and a hard bondage, and the slavery of market-places, and lawsuits, and crowds, instead of this freedom; and neither pleasure nor any sort of leisure shall remain to us for the pursuit of nobler objects. Neither shall we have to speak of the words of inspiration, but we shall have to speak of the works of men,—a thing which has been deemed simply a bane by the prophet,—and in our case, indeed, those of wicked men. And truly we shall have night in place of day, and darkness in place of the clear light, and grief instead of the festive assembly; and in place of a fatherland, a hostile country will receive us, in which I shall have no liberty to sing my sacred song, for how could I sing it in a land strange to my soul, in which the sojourners have no permission to approach God? but only to weep and mourn, as I call to mind the different state of things here, if indeed even that shall be in my power. We read that enemies once assailed a great and sacred city, in which the worship of God was observed, and dragged away its inhabitants, both singers and prophets, into their own country, which was Babylon. And it is narrated that these captives, when they were detained in the land, refused, even when asked by their conquerors, to sing the divine song, or to play in a profane country, and hung their harps on the willow-trees, and wept by the rivers of Babylon. Like one of these I verily seem to myself to be, as I am cast forth from this city, and from this sacred fatherland of mine, where both by day and by night the holy laws are declared, and hymns and songs and spiritual words are heard; where also there is perpetual sunlight; where by day in waking vision we have access to the mysteries of God, and by night in dreams we are still occupied with what the soul has seen and handled in the day; and where, in short, the inspiration of divine things prevails over all continually. From this city, I say, I am cast forth, and borne captive to a strange land, where I shall have no power to pipe: for, like these men of old, I shall have to hang my instrument on the willows, and the rivers shall be my place of sojourn, and I shall have to work in mud, and shall have no heart to sing hymns, even though I remember them; yea, it may be that, through constant occupation with other sub- jects, I shall forget even them, like one spoiled of memory itself. And would that, in going away, I only went away against my will, as a captive is wont to do; but I go away also of my own will, and not by constraint of another; and by my own act I am dispossessed of this city, when it is in my option to remain in it. Perchance, too, in leaving this place, I may be going to prosecute no safe journey, as it sometimes fares with one who quits some safe and peaceful city; and it is indeed but too likely that, in journeying, I may fall into the hands of robbers, and be taken prisoner, and be stripped and wounded with many strokes, and be cast forth to lie half-dead somewhere.

Argument XVII.—Gregory Consoles Himself.

But why should I utter such lamentations? There lives still the Savior of all men, even of the half-dead and the despoiled, the Protector and Physician for all, the Word, that sleepless Keeper of all. We have also seeds of truth which thou hast made us know as our possession, and all that we have received from thee,—those noble deposits of instruction, with which we take our course; and though we weep, indeed, as those who go forth from home, we yet carry those seeds with us. It may be, then, that the Keeper who presides over us will bear us in safety through all that shall befall as; and it may be that we shall come yet again to thee, bringing with us the fruits and handfuls yielded by these seeds, far from perfect truly, for how could they be so? but still such as a life spent in civil business makes it possible for us to rear, though marred indeed by a kind of faculty that is either unapt to bear fruit altogether, or prone to bear bad fruit, but which, I trust, is one not destined to be further misused by us, if God grants us grace.

Argument XVIII.— Peroration, and Apology for the Oration.

Wherefore let me now have done with this address, which I have had the boldness to deliver in a presence wherein boldness least became me. Yet this address is one which, I think, has aimed heartily at signifying our thanks to the best of our ability,—for though we have had nothing to say worthy of the subject, we could not be altogether silent,—and one, too, which has given expression to our regrets, as those are wont to do who go abroad in separation from friends. And whether this speech of mine may not have contained things puerile *or* bordering on flattery, or things offending by excess of simplicity on the one hand, or of elaboration on the other, I know not. Of this, however, I am clearly conscious, that at least there is in it nothing unreal, but all that is true and genuine, in sincerity of opinion, and in purity and integrity of judgment.

Argument XIX.—Apostrophe to Origen, and There with the Leave-Taking, and the Urgent Utterance of Prayer.

But, O dear soul, arise thou and offer prayer, and now dismiss us; and as by thy holy instructions thou hast been our rescuer when we enjoyed thy fellowship, so save us still by thy prayers in our separation. Commend us and set us constantly before thee in prayer. Or rather commend us continually to that God who brought us to thee, giving thanks for all that has been granted us in the past, and imploring Him still to lead us by the hand in the future, and to stand ever by us, filling our mind with the understanding of His precepts, inspiring us with the godly fear of Himself, and vouchsafing us henceforward His choicest guidance. For when we are gone from thee, we shall not have the same liberty for obeying Him as was ours when we were with thee. Pray, therefore, that some encouragement may be conveyed to us from Him when we lose thy presence, and that He may send us a good conductor, some angel to be our comrade on the way. And entreat Him also to turn our course, for that is the one thing which above all else will effectually comfort us, and bring us back to thee again.

Elucidations.
___

Neale, in his valuable work, does full justice to Dionysius, whose life is *twinned* with Gregory's; but he seems to me most unaccountably to slight the truly great and commanding genius of Gregory. I take opportunity, then, to direct attention to Neale's candid, and, on the whole, favorable view of Origen; but it grieves me whenever I see in critics a manifest inability to *put themselves back into the times* of which they write, as I think is the case, not infrequently, even with Dr. Neale. The figure of this grand ornament of the mighty patriarchate and school of Alexandria is colossal. His genius is Titanic, and has left all Christendom profoundly his debtor to this day, by the variety of his work and the versatility of his speech and pen. Doubtless the youthful Gregory's panegyric does contain, as he himself suggests, much that is "puerile or bordering on flattery;" but, as he protests with transparent truthfulness, "there is nothing in it unreal." It shines with "sincerity of thought and integrity of judgment." And as such, what a portrait it presents us of the love and patient effort of this lifelong confessor! Let me commend this example to professors of theology generally. All can learn from it the power of sweetness and love, united with holiness of purpose, to stamp the minds and the characters of youth with the divine "image and super- scription."

But, as to the sharpness of modern censures upon Origen's conspicuous faults, I must suggest three important considerations, which should be applied to all the Ante-Nicene doctors: (1) How could they who were working out the formulas of orthodoxy, be expected to use phrases with the skill and precision which became necessary only after the great Synodical period had embodied them in clear, dogmatic statements? (2) How could the active intellect of an Origen have failed to make great mistakes in such an immensity of la- bours and such a variety of works? (3) If, in our own day, we indulge speculative minds in large liberties so long as they never make shipwreck of the faith, how much more should we deem them excusable who were unable to consult libraries of well-digested thought, and to employ, as we do, the accumulated wealth of fifty generations of believers, whenever we are called to the solemn responsibility of impressing our convictions upon others? The conclusion of Dr. Neale's review of Origen balances the praise and blame accorded to him by those nearest to his times; but let us reflect upon the painful conflicts of those times, and upon the pressure under which, to justify their own positions, they were often forced to object to any error glorified by even the apparent patronage of Origen.

Part II.—Dubious or Spurious Writings.

A Sectional Confession of Faith.

I.

Most hostile and alien to the Apostolic Confession are those who speak of the Son as assumed to Himself by the Father out of nothing, and from an emanational origin; and those who hold the same sentiments with respect to the Holy Spirit; those who say that the Son is constituted divine by gift and grace, and that the Holy Spirit is made holy; those who regard the name of the Son as one common to servants, and assert that thus He is the first-born of the creature, as becoming, like the creature, existent out of non-existence, and as being first made, and who refuse to admit that He is the only-begotten Son,—the only One that the Father has, and that He has given Himself to be reckoned in the number of mortals, and is thus reckoned first-born; those who circumscribe the generation of the Son by the Father with a measured interval after the fashion of man, and refuse to acknowledge that the æon of the Begetter and that of the Begotten are without beginning; those who introduce three separate and diverse systems of divine worship, whereas there is but one form of legitimate service which we have received of old from the law and the prophets, and which has been confirmed by the Lord and preached by the apostles. Nor less alienated from the true confession are those who hold not the doctrine of the Trinity according to truth, as a relation consisting of three persons, but impiously conceive it as implying a triple being in a unity (Monad), formed in the way of synthesis and think that the Son is the wisdom in God, in the same manner as the human wisdom subsists in man whereby the man is wise, and represent the Word as being simply like the word which we utter or conceive, without any hypostasis whatever.

II.

But the Church's Confession, and the Creed that brings salvation to the world, is that which deals with the incarnation of the Word, and bears that He gave Himself over to the flesh of man which He acquired of Mary, while yet He conserved His own identity, and sustained no divine transposition or mutation, but was brought into conjunction with the flesh after the similitude of man; so that the flesh was made one with the divinity, the divinity having assumed the capacity of receiving the flesh in the fulfilling of the mystery. And after the dissolution of death there remained to the holy flesh a perpetual impassibility and a changeless immortality, man's original glory being taken up into it again by the power of the divinity, and being ministered then to all men by the appropriation of faith.

III.

If, then, there are any here, too, who falsify the holy faith, either by attributing to the divinity as its own what belongs to the humanity—progressions, and passions, and a glory coming with accession—or by separating from the divinity the progressive and passible body, as if subsisted of itself apart,—these persons also are outside the confession of the Church and of salvation. No one, therefore, can know God unless he apprehends the Son; for the Son is the wisdom by whose instrumentality all things have been created; and these created objects declare this wisdom, and God is recognized in the wisdom. But the wisdom of God is not anything similar to the wisdom which man possesses, but it is the perfect wisdom which proceeds from the perfect God, and abides forever, not like the thought of man, which passes from him in the word that is spoken and (straightway) ceases to be. Wherefore it is not wisdom only, but also God; nor is it Word only, but also Son. And whether, then, one discerns God through creation, or is taught to know Him by the Holy Scriptures, it is impossible either to apprehend Him or to learn of Him apart from His wisdom. And he who calls upon God rightly, calls on Him through the Son; and he who approaches Him in a true fellowship, comes to Him through Christ. Moreover, the Son Himself cannot be approached apart from the Spirit. For the Spirit is both the life and the holy formation of all things; and God sending forth this Spirit through the Son makes the creature like Himself.

IV.

One therefore is God the Father, one the Word, one the Spirit, the life, the sanctification of all. And neither is there another God as Father, nor is there another Son as Word of God, nor is there another Spirit as quickening and sanctifying. Further, although the saints are called both gods, and sons, and spirits, they are neither filled with the Spirit, nor are made like the Son and God. And if, then, any one makes this affirmation, that the Son is God, simply as being Himself filled with divinity, and not as being generated of divinity, he has belied the Word, he has belied the Wisdom, he has lost the knowledge of God; he has fallen away into the worship of the creature, he has taken up the impiety of the Greeks, to that he has gone back; and he has become a follower of the unbelief of the Jews, who, sup- posing the Word of God to be but a human son, have refused to accept Him as God, and have declined to acknowledge Him as the Son of God. But it is impious to think of the Word of God as merely human, and to think of the works which are done by Him as abiding, while He abides not Himself. And if anyone says that the Christ works all things only as commanded by the Word, he will both make the Word of God idle, and will change the Lord's order into servitude. For the slave is one altogether under command, and the created is not competent to create; for to suppose that what is itself created ma   n like manner create other things, would imply that it has ceased to be like the creature.

V.

Again, when one speaks of the Holy Spirit as an object made holy be able to apprehend all things as being sanctified in (the) Spirit. For he who has sanctified one, sanctifies all things. That man, consequently, belies the fountain of sanctification, the Holy Spirit, who denudes Him of the power of sanctifying, and he will thus be precluded from numbering Him with the Father and the Son; he makes nought, too, of the holy (ordinance of) baptism, and will no more be able to acknowledge the holy and august Trinity. For either we must apprehend the perfect Trinity in its natural and genuine glory, or we shall be under the necessity of speaking no more of a Trinity, but only of a Unity; or else, not numbering created objects with the Creator, nor the creatures with the Lord of all, we must also not number what is sanctified with what sanctifies; even as no object that is made can be numbered with the Trinity, but in the name of the Holy Trinity baptism and invocation and worship are administered. For if there are three several glories, there must also be three several forms of cultus with those who impiously worship the creature; for if there is a distinction in the nature of the objects worshipped, there ought to be also with these men a distinction in the nature of the worship offered. What is recent surely is not to be worshipped along with what is eternal; for the recent comprehends all that has had a beginning, while mighty and measureless is He who is before the ages. He, therefore, who supposes some beginning of times in the life of the Son and of the Holy Spirit, therewith also cuts off any possibility of numbering the Son and the Spirit with the Father. For as we acknowledge the glory to be one, so ought we also to acknowledge the substance in the Godhead to be one, and one also the eternity of the Trinity.

VI.

Moreover, the capital element of our salvation is the incarnation of the Word. We believe, therefore, that it was without any change in the Divinity that the incarnation of the Word took place with a view to the renewal of humanity. For there took place neither mutation nor transposition, nor any circumscription in will, as regards the holy energy of God; but while that remained in itself the same, it also effected the work of the incarnation with a view to the salvation of the world: and the Word of God, living on earth after man's fashion, maintained likewise in all the divine presence, fulfilling all things, and being united properly and individually with flesh; and while the sensibilities proper to the flesh were there, the *divine* energy maintained the impassibility proper to itself. Impious, therefore, is the man who introduces the passibility into the energy. For the Lord of glory appeared in fashion as a man when He undertook the economy upon the earth; and He fulfilled the law for men by His deeds, and by His sufferings He did away with man's sufferings, and by His death He abolished death, and by his resurrection He brought life to light; and now we look for His appearing from heaven in glory for the life and judgment of all, when the resurrection of the dead shall take place, to the end that recompense may be made to all according to their desert.

VII.

But some treat the Holy Trinity in an awful manner, when they confidently assert that there are not three persons, and introduce (the idea of) a person devoid of subsistence. Wherefore we clear ourselves of Sabellius, who says that the Father and the Son are the same. For he holds that the Father is He who speaks, and that the Son is the Word that abides in the Father, and becomes manifest at the time of the creation, and thereafter reverts to God on the fulfilling of all things. The same affirmation he makes also of the Spirit. We forswear this, because we believe that three persons—namely, Father, Son, and Holy Spirit—are declared to possess the one Godhead: for the one divinity showing itself forth according to nature in the Trinity establishes the oneness of the nature; and thus there is a (divinity that is the) property of the Father, according to the word, "There is one God the Father;" and there is a divinity hereditary in the Son, as it is written, "The Word was God;" and there is a divinity present according to nature in the Spirit—to wit, what subsists as the Spirit of God—according to Paul's statement, "Ye are the temple of God, and the Spirit of God dwelleth in you."

III.

Now the person in each declares the independent being and subsistence. But divinity is the property of the Father; and whenever the divinity of these three is spoken of as one, testimony is borne that the property of the Father belongs also to the Son and the Spirit: wherefore, if the divinity may be spoken of as one in three persons, the trinity is established, and the unity is not dissevered; and the oneness which is naturally the Father's is also acknowledged to be the Son's and the Spirit's. If one, however, speaks of one person as he may speak of one divinity, it cannot be that the two in the one are as one. For Paul addresses the Father as one in respect of divinity, and speaks of the Son as one in respect of lordship: "There is one God the Father, of whom are all things, and we for Him; and one Lord Jesus Christ, by whom are all things, and we by Him." Wherefore if there is one God, and one Lord, and at the same time one person as one divinity in one lordship, how can credit be given to (this distinction in) the words "of whom" and "by whom," as has been said before? We speak, accordingly, not as if we separated the lordship from the divinity, nor as estranging the one from the other, but as unifying them in the way warranted by actual fact and truth; and we call the Son God with the property of the Father, as being His image and offspring; and we call the Father Lord, addressing Him by the name of the One Lord, as being His Origin and Begettor.

IX.

The same position we hold respecting the Spirit, who has that unity with the Son which the Son has with the Father. Wherefore let the hypostasis of the Father be discriminated by the appellation of God; but let not the Son be cut off from this appellation, for He is of God. Again, let the person of the Son also be discriminated by the appellation of Lord; only let not God be dissociated from that, for He is Lord as being the Father of the Lord. And as it is proper to the Son to exercise lordship, for He it is that made (all things) by Himself, and now rules the things that were made, while at the same time the Father has a prior possession of that property, inasmuch as He is the Father of Him who is Lord; so we speak of the Trinity as One God, and yet not as if we made the one by a synthesis of three: for the subsistence that is constituted by synthesis is something altogether partitive and imperfect. But just as the designation Father is the expression of originality and generation, so the designation Son is the expression of the image and offspring of the Father. Hence, if one were to ask how there is but One God, if there is also a God of God, we would reply that that is a term proper to the idea of original causation, so far as the Father is the one First Cause. And if one were also to put the question, how there is but One Lord, if the Father also is Lord, we might answer that again by saying that He is so in so far as He is the Father of the Lord; and this difficulty shall meet us no longer.

X.

And again, if the impious say, How will there not be three Gods and three Persons, on the supposition that they have one and the same divinity?—we shall reply: Just because God is the Cause and Father of the Son; and this Son is the image and offspring of the Father, and not His brother; and the Spirit in like manner is the Spirit of God, as it is written, "God is a Spirit." And in earlier times we have this declaration from the prophet David: "By the word of the Lord were the heavens stablished, and all the power of them by the breath (spirit) of His mouth." And in the beginning of the book of the creation it is written thus: "And the Spirit of God moved upon the face of the waters." And Paul in his Epistle to the Romans says: "But ye are not in the flesh, but in the Spirit, if so be that the Spirit of God dwell in you." And again he says: "But if the Spirit of Him that raised up Jesus from the dead dwell in you, He that raised up Christ from the dead shall also quicken your mortal bodies by His Spirit that dwelleth in you." And again: "As many as are led by the Spirit of God, they are the sons of God. For ye have not received the spirit of bondage again to fear; but ye have received the Spirit of adoption, whereby we cry, Abba, Father." And again: "I say the truth in Christ, I lie not, my conscience also bearing me witness in the Holy Ghost." And again: "Now the God of hope fill you with all joy and peace in believing, that ye may abound in hope, by the power of the Holy Ghost."

XI.

And again, writing to those same Romans, he says: "But I have written the more boldly unto you in some sort, as putting you in mind, because of the grace that is given to me of God, that I should be the minister of Jesus Christ to the Gentiles, ministering the Gospel of God, that the offering up of the Gentiles might be acceptable, being sanctified by the Holy Ghost. I have therefore whereof I may glory through Jesus Christ in those things which pertain to God. For I dare not to speak of any of those things which Christ hath not wrought by me, to make the Gentiles obedient, by word and deed, through mighty signs and wonders, by the power of the Holy Spirit." And again: "Now I beseech you, brethren, for our Lord Jesus Christ's sake, and by the love of the Spirit." And these things, indeed, are written in the Epistle to the Romans.

XII.

Again, in the Epistle to the Corinthians he says: "For my speech and my preaching was not in the enticing words of man's wisdom, but in demonstration of the Spirit and of power; that your faith should not stand in the wisdom of men, but in the power of God." And again he says: "As it is written, Eye hath not seen, nor ear heard, neither have entered into the heart of man, the things which God hath prepared for them that love Him. But God hath revealed them unto us by His Spirit: for the Spirit searches all things, yea, the deep things of God. For what man knows the things of a man, save the spirit of man which is in him? Even so the things of God knows no man, but the Spirit of God." And again he says: "But the natural man receives not the things of the Spirit of God."

III.

Seest thou that all through Scripture the Spirit is preached, and yet nowhere named a creature? And what can the impious have to say if the Lord sends forth His disciples to baptize in the name of the Father, and of the Son, and of the Holy Spirit? Without contradiction, that implies a communion and unity between them, according to which there are neither three divinities nor (three) lordships; but, while there remain truly and certainly the three persons, the real unity of the three must be acknowledged. And in this way proper credit will be given to the *sending* and the *being sent* (in the Godhead), according to which the Father hath sent forth the Son, and the Son in like manner sends forth the Spirit. For one of the persons surely could not (be said to) send Himself; and one could not speak of the Father as incarnate. For the articles of our faith will not concur with the vicious tenets of the heresies; and it is right that our conceptions should follow the inspired and apostolic doctrines, and not that our impotent fancies should coerce the articles of our divine faith.

XIV.

But if they say, How can there be three Persons, and how but one Divinity?—we shall make this reply: That there are indeed three persons, inasmuch as there is one person of God the Father, and one of the Lord the Son, and one of the Holy Spirit; and yet that there is but one divinity, inasmuch as the Son is the Image of God the Father, who is One,—that is, He is God of God; and in like manner the Spirit is called the Spirit of God, and that, too, of nature according to the very substance, and not according to simple participation of God. And there is one substance in the Trinity, which does not subsist also in the case of objects that are made; for there is not one substance in God and in the things that are made, because none of these is in substance God. Nor, indeed, is the Lord one of these ac- cording to substance, but there is one Lord the Son, and one Holy Spirit; and we speak also of one Divinity, and one Lordship, and one Sanctity in the Trinity; because the Father is the Cause of the Lord, having begotten Him eternally, and the Lord is the Prototype of the Spirit. For thus the Father is Lord, and the Son also is God; and of God it is said that "God is a Spirit."

XV.

We therefore acknowledge one true God, the one First Cause, and one Son, very God of very God, possessing of nature the Father's divinity,—that is to say, being the same in substance with the Father; and one Holy Spirit, who by nature and in truth sanctifies all, and makes divine, as being of the substance of God. Those who speak either of the Son or of the Holy Spirit as a creature we anathematize. All other things we hold to be objects made, and in subjection, created by God through the Son, (and) sanctified in the Holy Spirit. Further, we acknowledge that the Son of God was made a Son of man, having taken to Himself the flesh from the Virgin Mary, not in name, but in reality; and that He is both the perfect Son of God, and the (perfect) Son of man,—that the Person is but one, and that there is one worship for the Word and the flesh that He assumed. And we anathematize those who constitute different worships, one for the divine and another for the human, and who worship the man born of Mary as though He were another than the God of God. For we know that "in the beginning was the Word, and the Word was with God, and the Word was God." And we worship Him who was made man on account of our salvation, not indeed as made perfectly like in the like body, but as the Lord who has taken to Himself the form of the servant. We acknowledge the passion of the Lord in the flesh, the resurrection in the power of His divinity, the ascension to heaven, and His glorious appearing when He comes for the judgment of the living and the dead, and for the eternal life of the saints.

VI.

And since some have given us trouble by attempting to subvert our faith in our Lord Jesus Christ, and by affirming of Him that He was not God incarnated, but a man linked with God; for this reason we present our confession on the subject of the aforementioned matters of faith, and reject the faithless dogmas opposed thereto. For God, having been incarnated in the flesh of man, retains also His proper energy pure, possessing a mind unsubjected by the natural and fleshly affections, and holding the flesh and the fleshly motions divinely and sinlessly, and not only unmastered by the power of death, but even destroying death. And it is the true God unincarnate that has appeared incarnate, the perfect One with the genuine and divine perfection; and in Him there are not two persons. Nor do we affirm that there are four to worship, viz., God and the Son of God, and man and the Holy Spirit. Wherefore we also anathematize those who show their impiety in this, and who thus give the man a place in the divine doxology. For we hold that the Word of God was made man on account of our salvation, in order that we might receive the likeness of the heavenly, and be made divine after the likeness of Him who is the true Son of God by nature, and the Son of man according to the flesh, our Lord Jesus Christ.

XVII.

We believe therefore in one God, that is, in one First Cause, the God of the law and of the Gospel, the just and good; and in one Lord Jesus Christ, true God, that is, Image of the true God, Maker of all things seen and unseen, Son of God and only-begotten Offspring, and Eternal Word, living and self-subsistent and active, always being with the Father; and in one Holy Spirit; and in the glorious advent of the Son of God, who of the Virgin Mary took flesh, and endured sufferings and death in our stead, and came to resurrection on the third day, and was taken up to heaven; and in His glorious appearing yet to come; and in one holy Church, the forgiveness of sins, the resurrection of the flesh, and life eternal.

XVIII.

We acknowledge that the Son and the Spirit are consubstantial with the Father, and that the substance of the Trinity is one,—that is, that there is one divinity according to nature, the Father remaining unbegotten, and the Son being begotten of the Father in a true generation, and not in a formation by will, and the Spirit being sent forth eternally from the substance of the Father through the Son, with power to sanctify the whole creation. And we further acknowledge that the Word was made flesh, and was manifested in the flesh- movement received of a virgin, and did not simply energize in a man. And those who have fellowship with men that reject the *consubstantiality* as a doctrine foreign to the Scriptures, and speak of any of the persons in the Trinity as created, and separate that person from the one natural divinity, we hold as aliens, and have fellowship with none such. There is one God the Father, and there is only one divinity. But the Son also is God, as being the true image of the one and only divinity, according to generation and the nature which He has from the Father. There is one Lord the Son; but in like manner there is the Spirit, who bears over the Son's lordship to the creature that is sanctified. The Son sojourned in the world, having of the Virgin received flesh, which He filled with the Holy Spirit for the sanctification of us all; and having given up the flesh to death, He destroyed death through the resurrection that had in view the resurrection of us all; and He ascended to heaven, exalting and glorifying men in Himself; and He comes the second time to bring us again eternal life.

XIX.

One is the Son, both before the incarnation and after the incarnation. The same (Son) is both man and God, both these together as though one; and the God the Word is not one person, and the man Jesus another person, but the same who subsisted as Son before was made one with flesh by Mary, so constituting Himself a perfect, and holy, and sinless man, and using that economical position for the renewal of mankind and the salvation of all the world. God the Father, being Himself the perfect Person, has thus the perfect Word begotten of Him truly, not as a word that is spoken, nor yet again as a son by adoption, in the sense in which angels and men are called sons of God, but as a Son who is in nature God. And there is also the perfect Holy Spirit supplied of God through the Son to the sons of adoption, living and life-giving, holy and imparting holiness to those who partake of Him,—not like an unsubstantial breath breathed into them by man, but as the living Breath proceeding from God. Wherefore the Trinity is to be adored, to be glorified, to be honored, and to be reverenced; the Father being apprehended in the Son even as the Son is of Him, and the Son being glorified in the Father, inasmuch as He is of the Father, and being manifested in the Holy Spirit to the sanctified.

XX.

And that the holy Trinity is to be worshipped without either separation or alienation, is taught us by Paul, who says in his Second Epistle to the Corinthians: "The grace of our Lord Jesus Christ, and the love of God, and the communion of the Holy Ghost, be with you all." And again, in that epistle he makes this explanation: "Now He which established us with you in Christ, and hath anointed us, is God, who hath also sealed us, and given the earnest of the Spirit in our hearts." And still more clearly he writes thus in the same epistle: "When Moses is read, the veil is upon their heart. Nevertheless when it shall turn to the Lord, the veil shall be taken away. Now the Lord is that Spirit; and where the Spirit of the Lord is, there is liberty. But we all with open face beholding as in a glass the glory of the Lord, are changed into the same image, from glory to glory, even as by the Spirit of the Lord."

XXI.

And again Paul says: "That mortality might be swallowed up of life. Now He that hath wrought us for the selfsame thing is God, who also hath given unto us the earnest of the Spirit." And again he says: "Approving ourselves as the ministers of God, in much patience, in afflictions, in necessities," and so forth. Then he adds these words: "By kindness, by the Holy Ghost, by love unfeigned, by the word of truth, by the power of God." Behold here again the saint has defined the holy Trinity, naming God, and the Word, and the Holy Ghost. And again he says: "Know ye not that ye are the temple of God, and that the Spirit of God dwelleth in you? If any man defiles the temple of God, him shall God destroy." And again: "But ye are washed, but ye are justified in the name of our Lord Jesus, and by the Spirit of our God." And again: "What! know ye not that your bodies are the temple of the Holy Ghost which is in you, which ye have of God?" "And I think also that I have the Spirit of God."

XXII.

And again, speaking also of the children of Israel as baptized in the cloud and in the sea, he says: "And they all drank of the same spiritual drink: for they drank of that spiritual Rock that followed them, and that Rock was

Christ." And again he says: "Wherefore I give you to understand, that no man speaking by the Spirit of God calleth Jesus accursed: and that no man can say that Jesus is the Lord, but by the Holy Ghost. Now there are diversities of gifts, but the same Spirit. And there are differences of administrations, but the same Lord. And there are diversities of operations, but it is the same God which worketh all in all. But the manifestation of the Spirit is given to every man to profit withal. For to one is given by the Spirit the word of wisdom; to another the word of knowledge by the same Spirit; to another faith by the same Spirit; to another the gifts of healing by the same Spirit; to another the working of miracles; to another prophecy; to another discerning of spirits; to another divers kinds of tongues; to another the interpretation of tongues: but all these worketh that one and the selfsame Spirit, dividing to every man severally as He will. For as the body is one, and hath many members, and all the members of that one body, being many, are one body; so also is Christ. For by one Spirit are we all baptized into one body." And again he says: "For if he who comes preaches another Christ whom we have not preached, or ye receive another spirit that ye have received not, or another gospel which ye have not obtained, ye will rightly be kept back."

XXIII.

Seest thou that the Spirit is inseparable from the divinity? And no one with pious apprehensions could fancy that He is a creature. Moreover, in the Epistle to the Hebrews he writes again thus: "How shall we escape, if we neglect so great salvation; which at the first began to be spoken by the Lord, and was confirmed unto us by them that heard Him; God also bearing them witness, both with signs and wonders, and with divers miracles, and gifts of the Holy Ghost?" And again he says in the same epistle: "Wherefore, as the Holy Ghost saith, Today, if ye will hear His voice, harden not your hearts, as in the provocation, in the day of temptation in the wilderness; when your fathers tempted me, proved me, and saw my works forty years. Wherefore I was grieved with that generation, and said, They do always err in their heart; for they have not known my ways: as I swear in my wrath, that they should not enter into my rest." And there, too, they ought to give ear to Paul, for he by no means separates the Holy Spirit from the divinity of the Father and the Son, but clearly sets forth the discourse of the Holy Ghost as one from the person of the Father, and thus as given expression to by God, just as it has been represented in the before-mentioned sayings. Wherefore the holy Trinity is believed to be one God, in accordance with these testimonies of Holy Scripture; albeit all through the inspired Scriptures numberless announcements are supplied us, all confirmatory of the apostolic and ecclesiastical faith.

A Fragment of the Same Declaration of Faith, Accompanied by Glosses.—From Gregory Thaumaturgus, as They Say, in His Sectional Confession of Faith.

To maintain two natures in the one Christ, makes a Tetrad of the Trinity, says he; for he expressed himself thus: "And it is the true God, the unincarnate, that was manifested in the flesh, perfect with the true and divine perfection, not with two natures; nor do we speak of worshipping four (persons), viz., God, and the Son of God, and man, and the Holy Spirit." First, however, this passage is misapprehended, and is of very doubtful import. Nevertheless it bears that we should not speak of two persons in Christ, lest, by thus acknowledging Him as God, and as in the perfect divinity, and yet speaking of two persons, we should make a Tetrad of the divine persons, counting that of God the Father as one, and that of the Son of God as one, and that of the man as one, and that of the Holy Spirit as one. But, again, it bears also against recognizing two divine natures, and rather for acknowledging Him to be perfect God in one natural divine perfection, and not in two; for his object is to show that He became incarnate without change, and that He retains the divinity without duplication. Accordingly he says shortly: "And while the affections of the flesh spring, the energy retains the impassibility proper to it. He, therefore, who introduces the (idea of) passion into the energy is impious; for it was the Lord of glory that appeared in human form, having taken to Himself the human economy."

Elucidations.

(The minister...to the Gentiles, p. 43.)
If St. Peter had been at Rome, St. Paul would not have come there (2 Cor. x. 16). The two apostles had each his jurisdiction, and they kept to their own "line of things"

respectively. How, then, came St. Peter to visit Rome? The answer is clear: unless he came involuntarily, as a prisoner, he came to look after the Church of the *Circumcision*, which was "in his measure;" and doubtless St. Paul urged him to this, the Hebrew Christians there being so large a proportion of the Church. St. Peter came "at the close of his life," doubtless attended by an apostolic companion, as St. Paul was, and Barnabas also (Acts xv. 39, 40). Linus probably labored for St. Paul (in prison) among the Gentile Romans, and Cletus for St. Peter among Jewish Christians. St. Peter *survived all his martyred associates*, and left Clement in charge of the whole Church. This most probable theory squares with all known facts, and reconciles all difficulties. Clement, then, was first bishop of Rome (a.d. 65); and so says Tertullian, vol. iii. p. 258, note 9.

That compendious but superficial little work, Smith's *History of the First Ten Centuries*, justly censures as "misleading" the usage, which it yet keeps up, of calling the early bishops of Rome "Popes." The same author utterly misunderstands Cyprian's references to Rome as "a principal *cathedra*," "*a* root and *matrix*," etc.; importing into the indefinite Latin *a definite article*. Cyprian applies a similar principle, after his master Tertullian (vol. iii. p. 260, this series), to all the Apostolic Sees, the *matrices* of Christian churches.

On the Trinity.

Fragment from the Discourse.

Gregory Thaumaturgus, Bishop of Neo-Cæsareia in Pontus, near successor of the apostles, in his discourse on the Trinity, speaks thus:—

I see in all three essentials—substance, genus, name. We speak of man, servant, curator (*curatorem*),—man, by reason of substance; servant, by reason of genus or condition; curator, by reason of denomination. We speak also of Father, Son, and Holy Spirit: these, however, are not names which have only supervened at some after period, but they are subsistences. Again, the denomination of *man* is not in actual fact a denomination, but a substance common to men, and is the denomination proper to all men. Moreover, names are such as these,—Adam, Abraham, Isaac, Jacob: these, I say, are names. But the Divine Persons are names indeed: and the names are still the persons; and the persons then signify that which is and subsists,—which is the essence of God. The name also of the nature signifies subsistence; as if we should speak of the *man*. All (the persons) are one nature, one essence, one will, and are called the Holy Trinity; and these also are names subsistent, one nature in three persons, and one genus. But the person of the Son is composite in its oneness (*unita est*), being one made up of two, that is, of divinity and humanity together, which two constitute one. Yet the divinity does not consequently receive any increment, but the Trinity remains as it was. Nor does anything new befall the people even or the names, but these are eternal and without time. No one, however, was sufficient to know these until the Son being made flesh manifested them, saying: "Father, I have manifested Thy name to men; glorify Thou me also, that they may know me as Thy Son." And on the mount the Father spoke, and said, "This is my beloved Son." And the same sent His Holy Spirit at the Jordan. And thus it was declared to us that there is an Eternal Trinity in equal honor. Besides, the generation of the Son by the Father is incomprehensible and ineffable; and because it is spiritual, its investigation becomes impracticable: for a spiritual object can neither be understood nor traced by a corporeal object, for that is far removed from human nature. We men know in- deed the generation proper to us, as also that of other objects; but a spiritual matter is above human condition, neither can it in any manner be understood by the minds of men. Spiritual substance can neither perish nor be dissolved; ours, however, as is easy to understand, perishes and is dissolved. How, indeed, could it be possible for man, who is limited on six sides—by east, west, south, north, deep, and sky—understand a matter which is above the skies, which is beneath the deeps, which stretches beyond the north and south, and which is present in every place, and fills all vacuity? But if, indeed, we are able to scrutinize spiritual substance, its excellence truly would be undone. Let us consider what is done in our body; and, furthermore, let us see whether it is in our power to ascertain in what manner thoughts are born of the heart, and words of the tongue, and the like. Now, if we can by no means apprehend things that are done in ourselves, how could it ever be that we should understand the mystery of the uncreated Creator, which goes beyond every mind? Assuredly, if this mystery were one that could be penetrated by man, the inspired John would by no means have affirmed this: "No man hath seen God at any time." He then, whom no man hath seen at any time,—whom can we reckon Him to resemble, so that thereby we should under- stand His generation? And we, indeed, without ambiguity apprehend that our soul dwells in us in union with the body; but still, who has ever seen his own soul? who has been able to discern its conjunction with his body? This one thing is all we know certainly, that there is a soul within us conjoined with the body. Thus, then, we reason and believe that the Word is begotten by the Father, albeit we neither possess nor know the clear *rationale* of the fact. The Word Himself is before every creature—eternal from the Eternal, like spring from spring, and light from light. The vocable *Word*, indeed, belongs to those three genera of words which are named in Scripture, and which are not substantial,—namely, the word *conceived*, the word *uttered*, and the word *articulated*. The word *conceived*, certainly, is not substantial. The word *uttered*, again, is that voice which the prophets hear from God, or the prophetic speech itself; and even this is not substantial. And, lastly, the word *articulated* is the speech of man formed forth in air (*aëre efformatus*), composed of terms, which also is not substantial. But the Word of God is substantial, endowed with an exalted and enduring nature, and is eternal with Himself, and is inseparable from Him, and can never fall away, but shall remain in an everlasting union. This Word created heaven and earth, and in Him were all things made. He is the arm and the power of God, never to be separated from the Father, in virtue of an indivisible nature, and, together with the Father, He is without beginning. This Word took our substance of the Virgin Mary; and in so far as He is spiritual indeed, He is indivisibly equal with the Father; but in so far as He is corporeal, He is in like manner inseparably equal with us. And, again, in so far as He is spiritual, He supplies in the same equality (*æquiparat*) the Holy Spirit, inseparably and without limit. Neither were there two natures, but only one nature of the Holy Trinity before the incarnation of the Word, the Son; and the nature of the Trinity remained one also after the incarnation of the Son. But if anyone, moreover, believes that any increment has been given to the Trinity by reason of the assumption of humanity by the Word, he is an alien from us, and from the ministry of the Catholic and Apostolic Church. This is the perfect, holy, Apostolic faith of the holy God. Praise to the Holy Trinity forever through the ages of the ages. Amen.

Elucidation.

Petavius, to whom the translator refers his readers, may be trusted in points where he has no theory of his own to sustain, but must always be accepted with caution. The Greek Fathers in this very series, from Justin onward, enable us to put the later terminology to the test of earlier exposition (see examples in the notes to the *Praxeas* of Tertullian, and consult Dr. Holmes' valuable note embodied in my elucidations). We may go back to Theophilus for the distinction between the ἐνδιάθετος and the προφορικός, the immanent and the uttered Word. Compare Tertullian, also, against Marcion. Evidences, therefore, are abundant and *archaic*, indeed, to prove that the Ante-Nicene Fathers, with those of the Nicene and the Post-Nicene periods, were of one mind, and virtually of one voice.

Twelve Topics on the Faith.
Wherein is Given Also the Formula of Excommunication, and an Explication is Sub- joined to Each.

Topic I.

If anyone says that the body of Christ is uncreated, and refuses to acknowledge that He, being the uncreated Word (God) of God, took the flesh of created humanity and appeared incarnate, even as it is written, let him be anathema.

Explication.

How could the body be said to be uncreated? For the uncreated is the passionless, invulnerable, intangible. But Christ, on rising from the dead, showed His disciples the print of the nails and the wound made by the spear, and a body that could be handled, although He also had entered among them when the doors were shut, with the view of showing them at once the energy of the divinity and the reality of the body.

Yet, while being God, He was recognized as man in a natural manner; and while subsisting truly as man, He was also manifested as God by His works.

Topic II.

If anyone affirms that the flesh of Christ is consubstantial with the divinity, and refuses to acknowledge that He, subsisting Himself in the form of God as God before all ages, emptied Himself and took the form of a servant, even as it is written, let him be anathema.

Explication.

How could the flesh, which is conditioned by time, be said to be consubstantial with the timeless divinity? For that is designated consubstantial which is the same in nature and in eternal duration without variableness.

Topic III.

If anyone affirms that Christ, just like one of the prophets, assumed the perfect man, and refuses to acknowledge that, being begotten in the flesh of the Virgin, He became man and was born in Bethlehem, and was brought up in Nazareth, and advanced in age, and on completing the set number of years (appeared in public and) was baptized in the Jordan, and received this testimony from the Father, "This is my beloved Son," even as it is written, let him be anathema.

Explication.

How could it be said that Christ (the Lord) assumed the perfect man just like one of the prophets, when He, being the Lord Himself, became man by the incarnation effected through the Virgin? Wherefore it is written, that "the first man was of the earth, earthy." But whereas he that was formed of the earth returned to the earth, He that became the second man returned to heaven. And so we read of the "first Adam and the last Adam." And as it is admitted that the second came by the first according to the flesh, for which reason also Christ is called man and the Son of man; so is the witness given that the second is the Savior of the first, for whose sake He came down from heaven. And as the Word came down from heaven, and was made man, and ascended again to heaven, He is on that account said to be the second Adam from heaven.

Topic IV.

If anyone affirms that Christ was born of the seed of man by the Virgin, in the same manner as all men are born, and refuses to acknowledge that He was made flesh by the Holy Spirit and the holy Virgin Mary, and became man of the seed of David, even as it is written, let him be anathema.

Explication.

How could one say that Christ was born of the seed of man by the Virgin, when the holy Gospel and the angel, in proclaiming the good tidings, testify of Mary the Virgin that she said, "How shall this be, seeing I know not a man?" Wherefore he says, "The Holy Ghost shall come upon thee, and the power of the highest shall overshadow thee: therefore also that holy thing which shall be born of thee shall be called the Son of the Highest And to Joseph he says, "Fear not to take unto thee Mary thy wife: for that which is conceived in her is of the Holy Ghost. And she shall bring forth a son, and they shall call His name Jesus: for He shall save His people from their sins."

Topic V.

If anyone affirms that the Son of God who is before the ages is one, and He who has appeared in these last times is another, and refuses to acknowledge that He who is before the ages is the same with Him who appeared in these last times, even as it is written, let him be anathema.

Explication.

How could it be said that the Son of God who is before the ages, and He who has appeared in these last times, are different, when the Lord Himself says, "Before Abraham was, I am;" and, "I came forth from God, and I come, and again I go to my Father?

Topic VI.

If anyone affirms that He who suffered is one, and that He who suffered not is another, and refuses to acknowledge that the Word, who is Himself the impassibie and unchangeable God, suffered in the flesh which He had assumed really, yet without mutation, even as it is written, let him be anathema.

Explication.

How could it be said that He who suffered is one, and He who suffered not another, when the Lord Himself says, "The Son of man must suffer many things, and be killed, and be raised again the third day from the dead;" and again, "When ye see the Son of man sitting on the right hand of the Father;" and again, "When the Son of man cometh in the glory of His Father?"

Topic VII.

If anyone affirms that Christ is saved, and refuses to acknowledge that He is the Savior of the world, and the Light of the world, even as it is written, let him be anathema.

Explication.

How could one say that Christ is saved, when the Lord Himself says, "I am the life;" and, "I am come that they might have life;" and, "He that believeth on me shall not see death, but he shall behold the life eternal?"

Topic VIII.

If anyone affirms that Christ is perfect man and also God the Word in the way of separation, and refuses to acknowledge the one Lord Jesus Christ, even as it is written, let him be anathema.

Explication.

How could one say that Christ is perfect man and also God the Word in the way of separation, when the Lord Himself says, "Why seek ye to kill me, a man that hath told you the truth, which I have heard of God?" For God the Word did not give a man for us, but He gave Himself for us, having been made man for our sake. Wherefore He says: "Destroy this temple, and in three days I will raise it up. But He spoke of the temple of His body.

Topic IX.

If anyone says that Christ suffers change or alteration, and refuses to acknowledge that He is unchangeable in the Spirit, though corruptible in the flesh, let him be anathema.

Explication.

How could one say that Christ suffers change or alteration, when the Lord Himself says, "I am and change not; again, "His soul shall not be left in Hades, neither shall His flesh see corruption?"

Topic X.

If anyone affirms that Christ assumed the man only in part, and refuses to acknowledge that He was made in all things like us, apart from sin, let him be anathema.

Explication.

How could one say that Christ assumed the man only in part, when the Lord Himsel says, "I lay down my life, that I might take it again, for the sheep;" and, "My flesh is meat indeed, and my blood is drink indeed;" and, "He that eats my flesh, and drinks my blood, hath eternal life?"

Topic XI.

If anyone affirms that the body of Christ is void of soul and understanding, and refuses to acknowledge that

He is perfect man, one and the same in all things (with us), let him be anathema.
Explication.

How could one say that the body of the Lord (Christ) is void of soul and understanding? For perturbation, and grief, and distress, are not the properties either of a flesh void of soul, or of a soul void of understanding; nor are they the sign of the immutable Divinity, nor the index of a mere phantasm, nor do they mark the defect of human weakness; but the Word exhibited in Himself the exercise of the affections and susceptibilities proper to us, having endued Himself with our passibility, even as it is written, that "He hath borne our griefs, and carried our sorrows." For perturbation, and grief, and distress, are disorders of soul; and toil, and sleep, and the body's liability to wounding, are infirmities of the flesh.

Topic XII.

If anyone says that Christ was manifested in the world only in semblance, and refuses to acknowledge that He came actually in the flesh, let him be anathema.

Explication.

How could one say that Christ was manifested only in semblance in the world, born as He was in Bethlehem, and made to submit to the circumcising of the flesh, and lifted up by Simeon, and brought up on to His twelfth year (at home), and made subject to His parents, and baptized in Jordan, and nailed to the cross, and raised again from the dead?

Wherefore, when it is said that He was "troubled in spirit, that "He was sorrowful in soul," that "He was wounded in body," He places before us designations of susceptibilities proper to our constitution, in order to show that He was made man in the world, and had His conversation with men, yet without sin. For He was born in Bethlehem according to the flesh, in a manner meet for Deity, the angels of heaven recognizing Him as their Lord, and hymning as their God Him who was then wrapped in swaddling-clothes in a manger, and exclaiming, "Glory to God in the highest, and on earth peace, good-will among men." He was brought up in Nazareth; but in divine fashion He sat among the doctors, and astonished them by a wisdom beyond His years, in respect of the capacities of His bodily life, as is recorded in the Gospel narrative. He was baptized in Jordan, not as receiving any sanctification for Himself, but as gifting a participation in sanctification to others. He was tempted in the wilderness, not as giving way, however, to temptation, but as putting our temptations before Himself on the challenge of the tempter, in order to show the powerlessness of the tempter.

Wherefore He says, "Be of good cheer, I have overcome the world." And this He said, not as holding before us any contest proper only to a God, but as showing our own flesh in its capacity to overcome suffering, and death, and corruption, in order that, as sin entered into the world by flesh, and death came to reign by sin over all men, the sin in the flesh might also be condemned through the selfsame flesh in the likeness thereof; and that that overseer of sin, the tempter, might be overcome, and death be cast down from its sovereignty, and the corruption in the burying of the body be done away, and the first-fruits of the resurrection be shown, and the principle of righteousness begin its course in the world through faith, and the kingdom of heaven be preached to men, and fellowship be established between God and men.

On behalf of this grace let us glorify the Father, who has given His only begotten Son for the life of the world. Let us glorify the Holy Spirit that works in us, and quickened us, and furnished the gifts meet for the fellowship of God; and let us not intermeddle with the word of the Gospel by lifeless disputations, scattering about endless questionings and logomachies, and making a hard thing of the gentle and simple word of faith; but rather let us work the work of faith, let us love peace, let us exhibit concord, let us preserve unity, let us cultivate love, with which God is well pleased.

As it is not for us to know the times or the seasons which the Father hath put in His own power,[428] but only to believe that there will come an end to time, and that there will be a manifestation of a future world, and a revelation of judgment, and an advent of the Son of God, and a recompense of works, and an inheritance in the kingdom of heaven, so it is not for us to know how the Son of God became man; for this is a great mystery, as it is written, "Who shall declare His generation? for His life is taken from the earth." But it is for us to believe that the Son of God became man, according to the Scriptures; and that He was seen on the earth, and had His conversation with men, according to the Scriptures, in their likeness, yet without sin; and that He died for us, and rose again from the dead, as it is written; and that He was taken up to heaven, and sat down at the right hand of the Father, whence He shall come to judge the quick and the dead, as it is written; lest, while we war against each other with words, any should be led to blaspheme the word of faith, and that should come to pass which is written, "By reason of you is my name continually blasphemed among the nations."

Elucidations.

These "twelve anathemas," as they are called, do evidently refute the Nestorians and later heretics. Evidently, therefore, we must assign this document to another author. And, as frequent references are made to such tests, I subjoin a list of Œcumenical or Catholic Councils, properly so called, as follows:—

1. Jerusalem, against *Judaism*, a.d. 50.
2. Nicæa, against *Arianism* (1), a.d. 325.
3. Constantinople (I.), against *Semi-Arianism* (2), a.d. 381.
4. Ephesus, against *Nestorianism* (3), a.d. 431.
5. Chalcedon, against *Eutychianism* (4), a.d. 451.
6. Constantinople (II.), against *Monophysitism* (5), a.d. 553.
7. Constantinople (III.), against *Monothelitism* (6), a.d. 680.

These are all *the undisputed* councils. The *Seventh Council*, so called (a.d. 537), was not a free council, and was rejected by a free council of the West, convened at Frankfort a.d. 794. Its acceptance by the Roman pontiffs, subsequently, should have no logical force with the Eastern, who do not recognize their supremacy even over the councils of the West; and no free council has ever been held under pontifical authority. The above list, therefore, is a complete list of all the councils of the undivided Church as defined by Catholic canons. There has been no possibility of a *Catholic* council since the division of East and West. The Council of Frankfort is the pivot of subsequent history, and its fundamental importance has not been sufficiently insisted upon.

On the Subject of the Soul.

You have instructed us, most excellent Tatian, to forward for your use a discourse upon the soul, laying it out in effective demonstrations. And this you have asked us to do without making use of the testimonies of Scripture,—a method which is opened to us, and which, to those who seek the pious mind, proves a manner of setting forth doctrine more convincing than any reasoning of man. You have said, however, that you desire this, not with a view to your own full assurance, taught as you already have been to hold by the Holy Scriptures and traditions, and to avoid being shaken in your convictions by any subtleties of man's disputations, but with a view to the confuting of men who have different sentiments, and who do not admit that such credit is to be given to the Scriptures, and who endeavor, by a kind of cleverness of speech, to gain over those who are unversed in such discussions. Wherefore we were led to comply readily with this commission of yours, not shrinking from the task on account of inexperience in this method of disputation, but taking encouragement from the knowledge of your goodwill toward us. For your kind and friendly disposition towards us will make you understand how to put forward publicly whatever you may approve of as rightly expressed by us, and to pass by and conceal whatever statement of ours you may judge to come short of what is proper. Knowing this, therefore, I have betaken myself with all confidence to the exposition. And in my discourse I shall use a certain order and consecution, such as those who are very expert in these matters employ towards those who desire to investigate any subject intelligently.

First of all, then, I shall propose to inquire by what criterion the soul can, according to its nature, be apprehended; then by what means it can be proved to exist; thereafter, whether it is a *substance* or an *accident*; then consequently on these points, whether it is a body or is incorporeal; then, whether it is simple or compound; next, whether it is mortal or immortal; and finally, whether it is rational or irrational.

For these are the questions which are wont, above all, to be discussed, in any inquiry about the soul, as most important, and as best calculated to mark out its distinctive nature. And as demonstrations for the establishing of these matters of investigation, we shall employ those common modes of consideration by which the credibility of matters under hand is naturally attested. But for the purpose of brevity and utility, we shall at present make use only of those modes of argumentation which are most cogently demonstrative on the subject of our inquiry, in order that clear and intelligible notions may impart to us some readiness for meeting the gainsayers. With this, therefore, we shall commence our discussion.

I. Wherein is the Criterion for the Apprehension of the Soul.

All things that exist are either known by sense or apprehended by thought. And what falls under sense has its adequate demonstration in sense itself; for at once, with the application, it creates in us the impression of what underlies it. But what is apprehended by thought is known not by itself, but by its operations. The soul, consequently, being unknown by itself, shall be known property by its effects.

II. Whether the Soul Exists.

Our body, when it is put in action, is put in action either from without or from within. And that it is not put in action from without, is manifest from the circumstance that it is put in action neither by impulsion nor by traction, like soulless things. And again, if it is put into action from within, it is not put into action according to nature, like fire. For fire never loses its action as long as there is fire; whereas the body, when it has become dead, is a body void of action. Hence, if it is put in action neither from without, like soulless things, nor according to nature, after the fashion of fire, it is evident that it is put in action by the soul, which also furnishes life to it. If, then, the soul is shown to furnish the life to our body, the soul will also be known for itself by its operations.

III. Whether the Soul is a Substance.

That the soul is a substance, is proved in the following manner. In the first place, because the definition given to the term substance suits it very well. And that definition is to the effect, that substance is that which, being ever identical, and ever one in point of numeration with itself, is yet capable of taking on contraries in succession. And that this soul, without passing the limit of its own proper nature, takes on contraries in succession, is, I fancy, clear to everybody. For righteousness and unrighteousness, courage and cowardice, temperance and intemperance, are seen in it successively;

and these are contraries. If, then, it is the property of a substance to be capable of taking on contraries in succession, and if the soul is shown to sustain the definition in these terms, it follows that the soul is a substance. And in the second place, because if the body is a substance, the soul must also be a substance. For it cannot be, that what only has life imparted should be a substance, and that what imparts the life should be no substance: unless one should assert that the non-existent is the cause of the existent; or unless, again, one were insane enough to allege that the dependent object is itself the cause of that very thing in which it has its being, and without which it could not subsist.

IV. Whether the Soul is Incorporeal.

That the soul is in our body, has been shown above. We ought now, therefore, to ascertain in what manner it is in the body. Now, if it is in juxtaposition with it, as one pebble with another, it follows that the soul will be a body, and also that the whole body will not be animated with soul, inasmuch as with a certain part it will only be in juxtaposition. But if again, it is mingled or fused with the body, the soul will become multiplex, and not simple, and will thus be despoiled of the rationale proper to a soul. For what is multiplex is also divisible and dissoluble; and what is dissoluble, on the other hand, is compound;[453] and what is compound is separable in a threefold manner. Moreover, body attached to body makes weight; but the soul, subsisting in the body, does not make weight, but rather imparts life. The soul, therefore, cannot be a body, but is incorporeal.

Again, if the soul is a body, it is put in action either from without or from within. But it is not put in action from without; for it is moved neither by impulsion nor by traction, like soulless things. Nor is it put in action from within, like objects animated with soul; for it is absurd to talk of a soul of the soul: it cannot, therefore, be a body, but it is incorporeal.

And besides, if the soul is a body, it has sensible qualities, and is maintained by nurture. But it is not thus nurtured. For if it is nurtured, it is not nurtured corporeally, like the body, but incorporeally; for it is nurtured by reason. It has not, therefore, sensible qualities: for neither is righteousness, nor courage, nor any one of these things, something that is seen; yet these are the qualities of the soul. It cannot, therefore, be a body, but is incorporeal.

Still further, as all corporeal substance is divided into animate and inanimate, let those who hold that the soul is a body tell us whether we are to call it animate or inanimate.

Finally, if every body has color, and quantity, and figure, and if there is not one of these qualities perceptible in the soul, it follows that the soul is not a body.

V. Whether the Soul is Simple or Compound.

We prove, then, that the soul is simple, best of all, by those arguments by which its in- corporeality has been demonstrated. For if it is not a body, while every body is compound, and what is composite is made up of parts, and is consequently multiplex, the soul, on the other hand, being incorporeal, is simple; since thus it is both uncompounded and indivisible into parts.

VI. Whether Our Soul is Immortal.

It follows, in my opinion, as a necessary consequence, that what is simple is immortal. And as to how that follows, hear my explanation: Nothing that exists is its own corrupter, else it could never have had any thorough consistency, even from the beginning. For things that are subject to corruption are corrupted by contraries: wherefore everything that is corrupted is subject to dissolution; and what is subject to dissolution is compound; and what is compound is of many parts; and what is made up of parts manifestly is made up of diverse parts; and the diverse is not the identical: consequently the soul, being simple, and not being made up of diverse parts, but being uncompound and indissoluble, must be, in virtue of that, incorruptible and immortal.

Besides, everything that is put in action by something else, and does not possess the principle of life in itself, but gets it from that which puts it in action, endures just so long as it is held by the power that operates in it; and whenever the operative power ceases, that also comes to a stand which has its capacity of action from it. But the soul, being self-acting, has no cessation of its being. For it follows, that what is self-acting is ever-acting; and what is ever-acting is unceasing; and what is unceasing is without end; and what is without end is incorruptible; and what is incorruptible is immortal. Consequently, if the soul is self-acting, as has been shown above, it follows that it is incorruptible and immortal, in accordance with the mode of reasoning already expressed.

And further, everything that is not corrupted by the evil proper to itself, is incorruptible; and the evil is opposed to the good, and is consequently its corrupter. For the evil of the body is nothing else than suffering, and disease, and death; just as, on the other hand, its excellency is beauty, life, health, and vigor. If, therefore, the soul is not corrupted by the evil proper to itself, and the evil of the soul is cowardice, intemperance, envy, and the like, and all these things do not despoil it of its powers of life and action, it follows that it is immortal.

VII. Whether Our Soul is Rational.

That our soul is rational, one might demonstrate by many arguments. And first of all from the fact that it has discovered the arts that are for the service of our life. For no one could say that these arts were introduced casually and accidentally, as no one could prove them to be idle, and of no utility for our life. If, then, these arts contribute to what is profitable for our life, and if the profitable is commendable, and if the commendable is constituted by reason, and if these things are the discovery of the soul, it follows that our soul is rational.

Again, that our soul is rational, is also proved by the fact that our senses are not sufficient for the apprehension of things. For we are not competent for the knowledge of things by the simple application of the faculty of sensation. But as we do not choose to rest in these without inquiry, that proves that the senses, apart from reason, are felt to be incapable of discriminating between things which are identical in form and similar in color, though quite distinct in their natures. If, therefore, the senses, apart from reason, give us a false conception of things, we have to consider whether things that are can be apprehended in reality or not. And if they can be apprehended, then the power which enables us to get at them is one different from, and superior to, the senses. And if they are not apprehended, it will not be possible for us at all to apprehend things which are different in their appearance from the reality. But that objects are apprehensible by us, is clear from the fact that we employ each in a way adaptable to utility, and again turn them to what we please. Consequently, if it has been shown that things which are can be apprehended by us, and if the senses, apart from reason, are an erroneous test of objects, it follows that the intellect is what distinguishes all things in reason, and discerns things as they are in their actuality. But the intellect is just the rational portion of the soul, and consequently the soul is rational.

Finally, because we do nothing without having first marked it out for ourselves; and as that is nothing else than just the high prerogative of the soul,—for its knowledge of things does not come to it from without, but it rather sets out these things, as it were, with the adornment of its own thoughts, and thus first pictures forth the object in itself, and only thereafter carries it out to actual fact,—and because the high prerogative of the soul is nothing else than the doing of all things with reason, in which respect it also differs from the senses, the soul has thereby been demonstrated to be rational.

Elucidations.
———————————— I.
(*Substance* or *accident*, p. 54.)

This essay is "rather the work of a philosopher than a bishop," says Dupin. He assigns it to an age when "Aristotle *began to be in some reputation*,"—a most important concession as to the estimate of this philosopher among the early faithful. We need not wonder that such admissions, honorable to his candor and to his orthodoxy, brought on him the hatred and persecutions of the Jesuits. Even Bossuet thought he went too far, and wrote against him. But the whole system of Roman dogma being grounded in Aristotle's *physics* as well as in his *metaphysics*, Dupin was not orthodox in the eyes of the society that framed Aristotle into a creed, and made it the creed of the "Roman-Catholic Church." Note, e.g., "transubstantiation," which is not true if Aristotle's theory of *accidents*, etc., is false. It assumes an exploded science.

II.

(Prerogative of the soul, p. 56.)

If this "Discourse" be worthy of study, it may be profitably contrasted, step by step, with Tertullian's treatises on kindred subjects. That the early Christians should reason concerning the Soul, the Mind, the immortal Spirit, was natural in itself. But it was also forced upon them by the "philosophers" and the heretics, with whom they daily came into conflict. This is apparent from the *Anti-Marcion* of the great Carthaginian. The annotations upon that treatise, and those *On the Soul's Testimony* and *On the Soul*, may suffice as pointing out the best sources of information on speculative points and their bearings on theology. Compare, however, Athenagoras and the great Clement of Alexandria.

Four Homilies

The First Homily.

On the Annunciation to the Holy Virgin Mary.

To-day are strains of praise sung joyfully by the choir of angels, and the light of the advent of Christ shines brightly upon the faithful. Today is the glad spring-time to us, and Christ the Sun of righteousness has beamed with clear light around us, and has illumined the minds of the faithful. To-day is Adam made anew, and moves in the choir of angels, having winged his way to heaven. To-day is the whole circle of the earth filled with joy, since the sojourn of the Holy Spirit has been realized to men. To-day the grace of God and the hope of the unseen shine through all wonders transcending imagination, and make the mystery that was kept hid from eternity plainly discernible to us. To-day are woven the chaplets of never-fading virtue. To-day, God, willing to crown the sacred heads of those whose pleasure is to hearken to Him, and who delight in His festivals, invites the lovers of unswerving faith as His called and His heirs; and the heavenly kingdom is urgent to summon those who mind celestial things to join the divine service of the incorporeal choirs. To-day is fulfilled the word of David, "Let the heavens rejoice, and let the earth be glad. The fields shall be joyful, and all the trees of the wood before the Lord, because He cometh." David thus made mention of the trees; and the Lord's forerunner also spoke of them as trees "that should bring forth fruits meet for repentance," or rather for the coming of the Lord. But our Lord Jesus Christ promises perpetual gladness to all those who believe on Him. For He says, "I will see you, and ye shall rejoice; and your joy no man taketh from you." To-day is the illustrious and ineffable mystery of Christians, who have willingly set their hope like a seal upon Christ, plainly declared to us. To-day did Gabriel, who stands by God, come to the pure virgin, bearing to her the glad annunciation, "Hail, thou that art highly favored!

And she cast in her mind what manner of salutation this might be. And the angel immediately proceeded to say, The Lord is with thee: fear not, Mary; for thou hast found favor with God. Behold, thou shalt conceive in thy womb, and bring forth a son, and shalt call His name Jesus. He shall be great, and shall be called the Son of the Highest; and the Lord God shall give unto Him the throne of His father David, and He shall reign over the house of Jacob forever: and of His kingdom there shall be no end. Then said Mary unto the angel, How shall this be, seeing I know not a man?" Shall I still remain a virgin? is the honor of virginity not then lost by me? And while she was yet in perplexity as to these things, the angel placed shortly before her the summary of his whole message, and said to the pure virgin, "The Holy Ghost shall come upon thee, and the power of the Highest shall overshadow thee; therefore also that holy thing which shall be born of thee shall be called the Son of God." For what it is, that also shall it be called by all means. Meekly, then, did grace make election of the pure Mary alone out of all generations. For she proved herself prudent truly in all things; neither has any woman been born like her in all generations. She was not like the primeval virgin Eve, who, keeping holiday alone in paradise, with thoughtless mind, unguardedly hearkened to the word of the serpent, the author of all evil, and thus became depraved in the thoughts of her mind; and through her that deceiver, discharging his poison and refusing death with it, brought it into the whole world; and in virtue of this has arisen all the trouble of the saints. But in the holy Virgin alone is the fall of that (first mother) repaired. Yet was not this holy one competent to receive the gift until she had first learned who it was that sent it, and what the gift was, and who it was that conveyed it. While the holy one pondered these things in perplexity with herself, she says to the angel, "Whence hast thou brought to us the blessing in such wise? Out of what treasure-stores is the pearl of the word dispatched to us? Whence has the gift acquired its purpose toward us? From heaven art thou come, yet thou walk upon earth! Thou dost exhibit the form of man, and (yet) thou art glorious with dazzling light." These things the holy one considered with herself, and the archangel solved the difficulty expressed in such reasonings by saying to her: "The Holy Ghost shall come upon thee, and the power of the Highest shall overshadow thee. Therefore also that holy thing which shall be born of thee shall be called the Son of God. And fear not, Mary; for I am not come to overpower thee with fear, but to repel the subject of fear. Fear not, Mary, for thou hast found favor with God. Question not grace by the standard of nature. For grace does not endure to pass under the laws of nature. Thou know, O Mary, things kept hid from the patriarchs and prophets. Thou hast learned, O virgin, things which were kept concealed till now from the angels. Thou hast heard, O purest one, things of which even the choir of inspired men was never deemed worthy. Moses, and David, and Isaiah, and Daniel, and all the prophets, prophesied of Him; but the manner they knew not. Yet thou alone, O purest virgin, art now made the recipient of things of which all these were kept in ignorance, and thou dost learn the origin of them. For where the Holy Spirit is, there are all things readily ordered. Where divine grace is present, all things are found possible with God. The Holy Ghost shall come upon thee, and the power of the Highest shall overshadow thee. Therefore also that holy thing which shall be born of thee shall be called the Son of God." And if He is the Son of God, then is He also God, of one form with the Father, and co-eternal; in Him the Father possesses all manifestation; He is His image in the person, and through His reflection the (Father's) glory shines forth. And as from the ever-flowing fountain the streams proceed, so also from this ever-flowing and ever-living fountain does the light of the world proceed, the perennial and the true, namely Christ our God. For it is of this that the prophets have preached: "The streams of the river make glad the city of God." And not one city only, but all cities; for even as it makes glad one city, so does it also the whole world. Appropriately, therefore, did the angel say to Mary the holy virgin first of all, "Hail, thou that art highly favored, the Lord is with thee;" inasmuch as with her was laid up the full treasure of grace. For of all generations she alone has risen as a virgin pure in body and in spirit; and she alone bears Him who bears all things on His word. Nor is it only the beauty of this holy one in body that calls forth our admiration, but also the innate virtue of her soul. Wherefore also the angel addressed her first with the salutation, "Hail, thou that art highly favored, the Lord is with thee, and no spouse of earth;" He Himself is with thee who is the Lord of sanctification, the Father of purity, the Author of incorruption, and the Bestower of liberty, the Curator of salvation, and the Steward and Provider of the true peace, who out of the virgin earth made man, and out of man's side formed Eve in addition. Even this Lord is with thee, and on the other hand also is of thee. Come, therefore, beloved brethren, and let us take up the angelic strain, and to the utmost of our ability return the due meed of praise, saying, "Hail, thou that art highly favored, the Lord is with thee!" For it is thine truly to rejoice, seeing that the grace of God, as he knows, has chosen to dwell with thee—the Lord of glory dwelling with the handmaiden; "He that is fairer than the children of men" with the fair *virgin*; He who sanctifies all things with the undefiled. God is with thee, and with thee also is the perfect man in whom dwells the whole fulness of the Godhead. Hail, thou that art highly favored, the fountain of the light that lightens all who believe upon Him! Hail, thou that art highly favored, the rising of the rational Sun, and the undefiled flower of Life! Hail, thou that art highly favored, the mead of sweet savor! Hail, thou that art highly favored, the ever-blooming vine, that makes glad the souls of those who honor thee! Hail, thou that art highly favored!—the soil that, all untilled, bears bounteous fruit: for thou hast brought forth in accordance with the law of nature indeed, as it goes with us, and by the set time of practice, and yet in a way beyond nature, or rather above nature, by reason that God the Word from above took His abode in thee, and formed the new Adam in thy holy womb, and inasmuch as the Holy Ghost gave the power of conception to the holy virgin; and the reality of His body was assumed from her body. And just as the pearl comes of the two natures, namely lightning and water, the occult signs of the sea; so also our Lord Jesus Christ proceeds, without fusion and without mutation, from the pure, and chaste, and undefiled, and holy Virgin Mary; perfect in divinity and perfect in humanity, in all things equal to the Father, and in all things consubstantial with us, apart from sin.

Most of the holy fathers, and patriarchs, and prophets desired to see Him, and to be eye-witnesses of Him, but did not attain hereto. And some of them by visions beheld Him in type, and darkly; others, again, were privileged to hear the divine voice through the medium of the cloud, and were favored with sights of holy angels; but to Mary the pure virgin alone did the archangel Gabriel manifest himself luminously, bringing her the glad address, "Hail, thou that art highly favored!" And thus she received the word, and in the due time of the fulfilment according to the body's course she brought forth the priceless pearl. Come, then, ye too, dearly beloved, and let us chant the melody which has been taught us by the inspired harp of David, and say, "Arise, O Lord, into Thy rest; Thou, and the ark of Thy sanctuary." For the holy Virgin is in truth an ark, wrought with gold both within and without, that has received the whole treasury of the sanctuary. "Arise, O Lord, into Thy rest." Arise, O Lord, out of the bosom of the Father, in order that Thou mayest raise up the fallen race of the first-formed man. Setting these things forth, David in prophecy said to the rod that was to spring from himself, and to sprout into the flower of that beauteous fruit, "Hearken, O daughter, and see, and incline thine ear, and forget thine own people and thy father's house; so shall the King greatly desire thy beauty: for He is the Lord thy God, and thou shalt worship Him." Hearken, O daughter, to the things which were prophesied beforetime of thee, in order that thou mayest also behold the things themselves with the eyes of understanding. Hearken to me while I announce things beforehand to thee, and hearken to the archangel who declares expressly to thee the perfect mysteries. Come then, dearly beloved, and let us fall back on the memory of what has gone before us; and let us glorify, and celebrate, and laud, and bless that rod that has sprung so marvelously from Jesse. For Luke, in the inspired Gospel narratives, delivers a testimony not to

Joseph only, but also to Mary the mother of God, and gives this account with reference to the very family and house of David: "For Joseph went up," says he, "from Galilee, unto a city of Judea which is called Bethlehem, to be taxed with Mary his espoused wife, being great with child, because they were of the house and family of David. And so it was, that while they were there, the days were accomplished that she should be delivered; and she brought forth her son, the first-born of the whole creation, and wrapped him in swaddling-clothes, and laid him in a manger, because there was no room for them in the inn." She wrapped in swaddling- clothes Him who is covered with light as with a garment. She wrapped in swaddling-clothes Him who made every creature. She laid in a manger Him who sits above the cherubim and is praised by myriads of angels. In the manger set apart for dumb brutes did the Word of God repose, in order that He might impart to men, who are really irrational by free choice, the perceptions of true reason. In the board from which cattle eat was laid the heavenly Bread, in order that He might provide participation in spiritual sustenance for men who live like the beasts of the earth. Nor was there even room for Him in the inn. He found no place, who by His word established heaven and earth; "for though He was rich, for our sakes He became poor," and chose extreme humiliation on behalf of the salvation of our nature, in His inherent goodness toward us. He who fulfilled the whole administration of unutterable mysteries of the economy in heaven in the bosom of the Father, and in the cave in the arms of the mother, reposed in the manger. Angelic choirs encircled Him, singing of glory in heaven and of peace upon earth. In heaven He was seated at the right hand of the Father; and in the manger

He rested, as it were, upon the cherubim. Even there was in truth His cherubic throne; there was His royal seat. Holy of the holy, and alone glorious upon the earth, and holier than the holy, was that wherein Christ our God rested. To Him be glory, honor, and power, together with the Father undefiled, and the altogether holy and quickening Spirit, now and ever, and unto the ages of the ages. Amen.

The Second Homily.
On the Annunciation to the Holy Virgin Mary. Discourse Second.

It is our duty to present to God, like sacrifices, all the festivals and hymnal celebrations; and first of all, the annunciation to the holy mother of God, to wit, the salutation made to her by the angel, "Hail, thou that art highly favored!" For first of all wisdom and saving doctrine in the New Testament was this salutation, "Hail, thou that art highly favored!" conveyed to us from the Father of lights. And this address, "highly favored," embraced the whole nature of men. "Hail, thou that art highly favored" in the holy conception and in the glorious pregnancy, "I bring you good tidings of great joy, which shall be to all people." And again the Lord, who came for the purpose of accomplishing a saving passion, said, "I will see you, and ye shall rejoice; and your joy no man taketh from you." And after His resurrection again, by the hand of the holy women, He gave us first of all the salutation "Hail!" And again, the apostle made the announcement in similar terms, saying, "Rejoice evermore: pray without ceasing: in everything give thanks." See, then, dearly beloved, how the Lord has conferred upon us everywhere, and indivisibly, the joy that is beyond conception, and perennial. For since the holy Virgin, in the life of the flesh, was in possession of the incorruptible citizenship, and walked as such in all manner of virtues, and lived a life more excellent than man's common standard; therefore the Word that cometh from God the Father thought it meet to assume the flesh, and endue the perfect man from her, in order that in the same flesh in which sin entered into the world, and death by sin, sin might be condemned in the flesh, and that the tempter of sin might be overcome in the burying of the holy body, and that therewith also the beginning of the resurrection might be exhibited, and life eternal instituted in the world, and fellowship established for men with God the Father. And what shall we state, or what shall we pass by here? or who shall explain what is incomprehensible in the mystery? But for the present let us fall back upon our subject. Gabriel was sent to the holy virgin; the incorporeal was dispatched to her who in the body pursued the incorruptible conversation, and lived in purity and in virtues. And when he came to her, he first addressed her with the salutation, "Hail, thou that art highly favored! the Lord is with thee." Hail, thou that art highly favored! for thou does what is worthy of joy indeed, since thou hast put on the vesture of purity, and art girt with the cincture of prudence. Hail, thou that art highly favored! for to thy lot it has fallen to be the vehicle of celestial joy. Hail, thou that art highly favored! for through thee joy is decreed for the whole creation, and the human race receives again by thee its pristine dignity. Hail, thou that art highly favored! for in thy arms the Creator of all things shall be carried. And she was perplexed by this word; for she was inexperienced in all the addresses of men, and welcomed quiet, as the mother of prudence and purity; (yet) being a pure, and immaculate, and stainless image herself, she shrank not in terror from the angelic apparition, like most of the prophets, as indeed true virginity has a kind of affinity and equality with the angels. For the holy Virgin guarded carefully the torch of virginity, and gave diligent heed that it should not be extinguished or defiled. And as one who is clad in a brilliant robe deems it a matter of great moment that no impurity or filth be suffered to touch it anywhere, so did the holy Mary consider with herself, and said: Does this act of attention imply any deep design or seductive purpose? Shall this word "Hail" prove the cause of trouble to me, as of old the fair promise of being made like God, which was given her by the serpent-devil, proved to our first mother Eve? Has the devil, who is the author of all evil, become transformed again into an angel of light; and bearing a grudge against my espoused husband for his admirable temperance, and having assailed him with some fair-seeming address, and finding himself powerless to overcome a mind so firm, and to deceive the man, has he turned his attack upon me, as one endowed with a more susceptible mind; and is this word "Hail" (Grace be with thee) spoken as the sign of gracelessness hereafter? Is this benediction and salutation uttered in irony? Is there not some poison concealed in the honey? Is it not the address of one who brings good tidings, while the end of the same is to make me the designer's prey? And how is it that he can thus salute one whom he knows not? These things she pondered in perplexity with herself, and expressed in words. Then again the archangel addressed her with the announcement of a joy which all may believe in, and which shall not be taken away, and said to her, "Fear not, Mary, for thou hast found favor with God." Shortly hast thou the proof of what has been said. For I not only give you to understand that there is nothing to fear, but I show you the very key to the absence of all cause for fear. For through me all the heavenly powers hail thee, the holy virgin: yea rather, He Himself, who is Lord of all the heavenly powers and of all creation, has selected thee as the holy one and the wholly fair; and through thy holy, and chaste, and pure, and undefiled womb the enlightening Pearl comes forth for the salvation of all the world: since of all the race of man thou art by birth the holy one, and the more honorable, and the purer, and the more pious than any other: and thou hast a mind whiter than the snow, and a body made purer than any gold, however fine, and a womb such as the object which Ezekiel saw, and which he has described in these terms: "And the likeness of the living creatures upon the head was as the firmament, and as the appearance of the terrible crystal, and the likeness of the throne above them was as the appearance of a sapphire-stone: and above the throne it was as the likeness of a man, and as the appearance of amber; and within it there was, as it were, the likeness of fire round about."

Clearly, then, did the prophet behold in type Him who was born of the holy virgin, whom thou, O holy virgin, would have had no strength to bear, had thou not beamed forth for that time with all that is glorious and virtuous. And with what words of laudation, then, shall we describe her virgin-dignity? With what indications and proclamations of praise shall we celebrate her stainless figure? With what spiritual song or word shall we honor her who is most glorious among the angels? She is planted in the house of God like a fruitful olive that the Holy Spirit overshadowed; and by her means are we called sons and heirs of the kingdom of Christ. She is the ever-blooming paradise of incorruptibility, wherein is planted the tree that giveth life, and that furnished to all the fruits of immortality. She is the boast and glory of virgins, and the exultation of mothers. She is the sure support of the believing, and the succorer of the pious. She is the vesture of light, and the domicile of virtue. She is the ever-flowing fountain, wherein the water of life sprang and produced the Lord's incarnate manifestation. She is the monument of righteousness; and all who be- come lovers of her, and set their affections on virgin-like ingenuousness and purity, shall enjoy the grace of angels. All who keep themselves from wine and intoxication, and from the wanton enjoyments of strong drink, shall be made glad with the products of the life- bearing plant. All who have preserved the lamp of virginity unextinguished shall be privileged to receive the amaranthine crown of immortality. All who have possessed themselves of the stainless robe of temperance shall be received into the mystical bride-chamber of righteous- ness. All who have come nearer the angelic degree than others shall also enter into the more real enjoyment of their Lord's beatitude. All who have possessed the illuminating oil of understanding, and the pure incense of conscience, shall inherit the promise of spiritual favor and the spiritual adoption. All who worthily observe the festival of the Annunciation of the Virgin Mary, the mother of God, acquire as their meet recompense the fuller interest in the message, "Hail, thou that art highly favored!" It is our duty, therefore, to keep this feast, seeing that it has filled the whole world with joy and gladness. And let us keep it with psalms, and hymns, and spiritual songs. Of old did Israel also keep their festival, but then it was with unleavened bread and bitter herbs, of which the prophet says: "I will turn their feasts into afflictions and lamentation, and their joy into shame." But our afflictions our Lord has assured us He will turn into joy by the fruits of penitence. And again, the first covenant maintained the righteous requirements of a divine service, as in the case of our forefather Abraham; but these stood in the inflictions of pain in the flesh by circumcision, until the time of the fulfilment. "The law was given to them through Moses" for their discipline; "but grace and truth" have been given to us by Jesus Christ. The beginning of all these blessings to us appeared in the annunciation to Mary, the highly-favored, in the economy of the Savior which is worthy of all praise, and in His divine and supra-mundane instruction. Thence rise the rays of the light of understanding upon us. Thence spring for us the fruits of wisdom and immortality, sending forth the clear pure streams of piety. Thence come to us the brilliant splendors of the treasures of divine knowledge. "For this is life eternal, that we may know the true God, and Jesus Christ whom He hath sent." And again, "Search the Scriptures, for in them ye think ye have eternal life." For on this account the treasure of the knowledge of God is revealed to them who search the divine oracles. That treasure of the inspired Scriptures the Paraclete has unfolded to us this day. And let the tongue of prophecy and the doctrine of apostles be the treasure of wisdom to us; for without the law and the prophets, or the evangelists and the apostles, it is not possible to have the certain hope of salvation. For by the tongue of the holy prophets and apostles our Lord speaks, and God takes pleasure in the words of the saints; not that He requires the spoken address, but that He delights in the good disposition; not that He receives any profit from men, but that He finds a restful satisfaction in the rightly-affected soul of the righteous. For it is not that Christ is magnified by what we say; but as we receive benefits from Him, we proclaim with grateful mind His beneficence to us; not that we can attain to what is worthy therein, but that we give the meet return to the best of our ability. And when the Gospels or the Epistles, therefore, are read, let not your attention center on the book or on the reader, but on the God who speaks to you from heaven. For the book is but that which is seen, while Christ is the divine subject spoken of. It brings us then the glad tidings of that economy of the Savior, which is worthy of all praise, to wit, that, though He was God, He became man through kindness toward man, and did not lay aside, indeed, the dignity which was His from all eternity, but assumed the economy that should work salvation. It brings us the glad tidings of that economy of the Savior worthy of all praise, to wit, that He sojourned with us as a physician for the sick, who did not heal them with potions, but restored them by the inclination of His philanthropy.

It brings us the glad tidings of this economy of the Savior altogether to be praised, to wit, that to them who had wandered astray the way of salvation was shown, and that to the despairing the grace of salvation was made known, which blesses all in different modes; searching after the erring, enlightening the blinded, giving life to the dead, setting free the slaves, redeeming the captives, and becoming all things to all of us in order to be the true way of salvation to us: and all this He does, not by reason of our goodwill toward Him, but in virtue of a benignity that is proper to our Benefactor Himself. For the Savior did all, not in order that He might acquire virtue Himself, but that He might put us in possession of eternal life. He made man, indeed, after the image of God, and appointed him to live in a paradise of pleasure. But the man being deceived by the devil, and having become a transgressor of the divine commandment, was made subject to the doom of death. Whence, also, those born of him were involved in their father's liability in virtue of their succession, and had the reckoning of condemnation required of them. "For death reigned from Adam to Moses." But the Lord, in His benignity toward man, when He saw the creature He Himself had formed now held by the power of death, did not turn away finally from him whom He had made in His own image, but visited him in each generation, and forsook him not; and manifesting Himself first of all among the patriarchs, and then proclaiming Himself in the law, and presenting the likeness of Himself in the prophets, He presignified the economy of salvation. When, moreover, the fulness of the times came for His glorious appearing, He sent beforehand the archangel Gabriel to bear the glad tidings to the Virgin Mary. And he came down from the ineffable powers above to the holy Virgin, and addressed her first of all with the salutation, "Hail, thou that art highly favored." And when this word, "Hail, thou that art highly favored," reached her, in the very moment of her hearing it, the Holy Spirit entered into the undefiled temple of the Virgin, and her mind and her members were sanctified together. And nature stood opposite, and natural intercourse at a distance, beholding with amazement the Lord of nature, in a manner contrary to nature, or rather above nature, doing a miraculous work in the body; and by the very weapons by which the devil strove against us, Christ also saved us, taking to Himself our passible body in order that He might impart the greater grace to the being who was deficient in it. And "where sin abounded, grace did much more abound." And appropriately was grace sent to the holy Virgin. For this word also is contained in the oracle of the evangelic history: "And in the sixth month the angel Gabriel was sent to a virgin espoused to a man whose name was Joseph, of the house and lineage of David; and the virgin's name was Mary;" and so forth. And this was the first month to the holy Virgin. Even as Scripture says in the book of the law: "This month shall be unto you the beginning of months: it shall be the first month among the months of the year to you." "Keep ye the feast of the holy Passover to the Lord in all your generations." It was also the sixth month to Zacharias. And rightly, then, did the holy Virgin prove to be of the family of David, and she had her home in Bethlehem, and was betrothed rightfully to Joseph, in accordance with the laws of relationship. And her espoused husband was her guardian, and possessor also of the untarnished incorruption which was hers. And the name given to the holy Virgin was one that became her exceedingly. For she was called Mary, and that, by interpretation, means *illumination*. And what shines more brightly than the light of virginity? For this reason also the virtues are called virgins by those who strive rightly to get at their true nature. But if it is so great a blessing to have a virgin heart, how great a boon will it be to have the flesh that cherishes virginity along with the soul!

Thus the holy Virgin, while still in the flesh, maintained the incorruptible life, and received in faith the things which were announced by the archangel. And thereafter she journeyed diligently to her relation Elisabeth in the hill-country. "And she entered into the house of Zacharias, and saluted Elisabeth," in imitation of the angel.

"And it came to pass, that, when Elisabeth heard the salutation of Mary, the babe leapt with joy in her womb; and Elisabeth was filled with the Holy Ghost." Thus the voice of Mary wrought with power, and filled Elisabeth with the Holy Ghost. And by her tongue, as from an ever-flowing fountain, she sent forth a stream of gracious gifts in the way of prophecy to her relation; and while the feet of her child were bound in the womb, she prepared to dance and leap. And that was the sign of marvelous jubilation. For wherever she was who was highly favored, there she filled all things with joy. "And Elisabeth spoke out with a loud voice, and said, Blessed art thou among women, and blessed is the fruit of thy womb. And whence is this to me, that the mother of my Lord should come to me? Blessed art thou among women." For thou hast become to women the beginning of the new creation. Thou hast given to us boldness of access into paradise, and thou hast put to flight our ancient woe. For after thee the race of woman shall no more be made the subject of reproach. No more do the successors of Eve fear the ancient curse, or the pangs of childbirth. For Christ, the Redeemer of our race, the Savior of all nature, the spiritual Adam who has healed the hurt of the creature of earth, cometh forth from thy holy womb. "Blessed art thou among women, and blessed is the fruit of thy womb." For He who bears all blessings for us is manifested as thy fruit. This we read in the clear words of her who was barren; but yet more clearly did the holy Virgin herself express this again when she presented to God the song replete with thanksgiving, and acceptance, and divine knowledge; announcing ancient things together with what was new; proclaiming along with things which were of old, things also which belong to the consummation of the ages; and summing up in a short discourse the mysteries of Christ. "And Mary said, My soul doth magnify the Lord, and my spirit hath rejoiced in God my Savior," and so forth. "He hath holpen His servant Israel in remembrance of His mercy, and of the covenant which He established with Abraham and with his seed forever." Thou sees how the holy Virgin has surpassed even the perfection of the patriarchs, and how she confirms the covenant which was made with Abraham by God, when He said, "This is the covenant which I shall establish between me and thee." Wherefore He has come and confirmed the covenant with Abraham, having received mystically in Himself the sign of circumcision, and having proved Himself the fulfilment of the law and the prophets. This song of prophecy, therefore, did the holy mother of God render to God, saying, "My soul doth magnify the Lord, and my spirit hath rejoiced in God my Savior: for He that is mighty hath done to me great things, and holy is His name." For having made me the mother of God, He has also preserved me a virgin; and by my womb the fulness of all generations is headed up together for sanctification. For He hath blessed every age, both men and women, both young men and youths, and old men. "He hath made strength with His arm,"[539] on our behalf, against death and against the devil, having torn the handwriting of our sins. "He hath scattered the proud in the imagination of their hearts;" yea, He hath scattered the devil himself, and all the demons that serve under him. For he was overweeningly haughty in his heart, seeing that he dared to say, "I will set my throne above the clouds, and I will be like the Most High." And now, how He scattered him the prophet has indicated in what follows, where he says, "Yet now thou shalt be brought down to hell," and all thy hosts with thee. For He has overthrown everywhere his altars and the worship of vain gods, and He has prepared for Himself a peculiar people out of the heathen nations. "He hath put down the mighty from their seats, and exalted them of low degree." In these terms is intimated in brief the extrusion of the Jews and the admission of the Gentiles. For the elders of the Jews and the scribes in the law, and those who were richly privileged with other prerogatives, because they used their riches ill and their power lawlessly, were cast down by Him from every seat, whether of prophecy or of priesthood, whether of legislature or of doctrine, and were stripped of all their ancestral wealth, and of their sacrifices and multitudinous festivals, and of all the honorable privileges of the kingdom. Spoiled of all these boons, as naked fugitives they were cast out into captivity. And in their stead the humble were exalted, namely, the Gentile peoples who hungered after righteousness. For, discovering their own lowliness, and the hunger that pressed upon them for the knowledge of God, they pleaded for the divine word, though it were but for crumbs of the same, like the woman of Canaan; and for this reason they were filled with the riches of the divine mysteries. For the Christ who was born of the Virgin, and who is our God, has given over the whole inheritance of divine blessings to the Gentiles. "He hath holpen His servant Israel." Not any Israel in general, indeed, but His servant, who in very deed maintains the true nobility of Israel. And on this account also did the mother of God call Him servant (Son) and heir. For when He had found the same laboring painfully in the letter and the law, He called him by grace. It is such an Israel, therefore, that He called and hath holpen in remembrance of His mercy. "As

He spoke to our fathers, to Abraham and to his seed forever." In these few words is comprehended the whole mystery of the economy. For, with the purpose of saving the race of men, and fulfilling the covenant that was made with our fathers, Christ has once "bowed the heavens and come down." And thus He shows Himself to us as we are capable of receiving Him, in order that we might have power to see Him, and handle Him, and hear Him when the speaks. And on this account did God the Word deem it meet to take to Himself the flesh and the perfect humanity by a woman, the holy Virgin; and He was born a man, in order that He might discharge our debt, and fulfil even in Himself the ordinances of the covenant made with Abraham, in its rite of circumcision, and all the other legal appointments connected with it. And after she had spoken these words the holy Virgin went to Nazareth; and from that a decree of Cæsar led her to come again to Bethlehem; and so, as proceeding herself from the royal house, she was brought to the royal house of David along with Joseph her espoused husband. And there ensued there the mystery which transcends all wonders,—the Virgin brought forth and bore in her hand Him who bears the whole creation by His word. "And there was no room for them in the inn." He found no room who founded the whole earth by His word. She nourished with her milk Him who imparts sustenance and life to everything that hath breath. She wrapped Him in swaddling-clothes who binds the whole creation fast with His word. She laid Him in a manger who rides seated upon the cherubim. A light from heaven shone round about Him who lightened the whole creation. The hosts of heaven attended Him with their doxologies who is glorified in heaven from before all ages. A star with its torch guided them who had come from the distant parts of earth toward Him who is the true Orient. From the East came those who brought gifts to Him who for our sakes became poor. And the holy mother of God kept these words, and pondered them in her heart, like one who was the receptacle of all the mysteries. Thy praise, O most holy Virgin, surpasses all laudation, by reason of the God who received the flesh and was born man of thee. To thee every creature, of things in heaven, and things on earth, and things under the earth, offers the meet offering of honor. For thou hast been indeed set forth as the true cherubic throne. Thou shines as the very brightness of light in the high places of the kingdoms of intelligence; where the Father, who is without beginning, and whose power thou had overshadowing thee, is glorified; where also the Son is worshipped, whom thou didst bear according to the flesh; and where the Holy Spirit is praised, who effected in thy womb the generation of the mighty King. Through thee, O thou that art highly favored, is the holy and consubstantial Trinity known in the world. Together with thyself, deem us also worthy to be made partakers of thy perfect grace in Jesus Christ our Lord: with whom, and with the Holy Spirit, be glory to the Father, now and ever, and unto the ages of the ages. Amen.

The Third Homily.
On the Annunciation to the Holy Virgin Mary.

Again have we the glad tidings of joy, again the announcements of liberty, again the restoration, again the return, again the promise of gladness, again the release from slavery. An angel talks with the Virgin, in order that the serpent may no more have converse with the woman.

In the sixth month, it is said, the angel Gabriel was sent from God to a virgin espoused to a man. Gabriel was sent to declare the world-wide salvation: Gabriel was sent to bear to Adam the signature of his restoration; Gabriel was sent to a virgin, in order to transform the dishonor of the female sex into honor; Gabriel was sent to prepare the worthy chamber for the pure spouse; Gabriel was sent to wed the creature with the Creator; Gabriel was sent to the animate palace of the King of the angels; Gabriel was sent to a virgin espoused to Joseph, but preserved for Jesus the Son of God. The incorporeal servant was sent to the virgin undefiled. One free from sin was sent to one that admitted no corruption. The light was sent that should announce the Sun of righteousness. The dawn was sent that should precede the light of the day. Gabriel was sent to proclaim Him who is in the bosom of the Father, and who yet was to be in the arms of the mother. Gabriel was sent to declare Him who is upon the throne, and yet also in the cavern. The subaltern was sent to utter aloud the mystery of the great King; the mystery, I mean, which is discerned by faith, and which cannot be searched out by officious curiosity; the mystery which is to be adored, not weighed; the mystery which is to be taken as a thing divine, and not measured. "In the sixth month Gabriel was sent to a virgin." What is meant by this sixth month? What? It is the sixth month from the time when Elisabeth received the glad tidings, from the time that she conceived John. And how is this made plain? The archangel himself gives us the interpretation, when he says to the virgin: "Behold, thy relation Elisabeth, she hath also conceived a son in her old age: and this is now the sixth month with her, who was called barren." In the sixth month—that is evidently, therefore, the sixth month of the conception of

John. For it was meet that the subaltern should go before; it was meet that the attendant should precede; it was meet that the herald of the Lord's coming should prepare the way for Him. In the sixth month the angel Gabriel was sent to a virgin espoused to a man; espoused, not united; espoused, yet kept intact. And for what purpose was she espoused? In order that the spoiler might not learn the mystery prematurely. For that the King was to come by a virgin, was a fact known to the wicked one. For he too heard these words of Isaiah: "Behold, a virgin shall conceive, and bear a son." And on every occasion, consequently, he kept watch upon the virgin's words, in order that, whenever this mystery should be fulfilled, he might prepare her dishonor. Wherefore the Lord came by an espoused virgin, in order to elude the notice of the wicked one; for one who was espoused was pledged in fine to be her husband's. "In the sixth month the angel Gabriel was sent to a virgin espoused to a man whose name was Joseph." Hear what the prophet says about this man and the virgin: "This book that is sealed shall be delivered to a man that is learned." What is meant by this sealed book, but just the virgin undefiled? From whom is this to be given? From the priests evidently. And to whom? To the artisan Joseph. As, then, the priests espoused Mary to Joseph as to a prudent husband, and committed her to his care in expectation of the time of marriage, and as it behooved him then on obtaining her to keep the virgin untouched, this was announced by the prophet long before, when he said: "This book that is sealed shall be delivered to a man that is learned." And that man will say, I cannot read it. But why canst thou not read it, O Joseph? I cannot read it, he says, because the book is sealed. For whom, then, is it pre- served? It is preserved as a place of sojourn for the Maker of the universe. But let us return to our immediate subject. In the sixth month Gabriel was sent to a virgin—he who received, indeed, such injunctions as these: "Come hither now, archangel, and become the minister of a dread mystery which has been kept hid, and be thou the agent in the miracle. I am moved by my compassions to descend to earth in order to recover the lost Adam. Sin hath made him decay who was made in my image, and hath corrupted the work of my hands, and hath obscured the beauty which I formed. The wolf devours my nursling, the home of paradise is desolate, the tree of life is guarded by the flaming sword, the location of enjoyments is closed. My pity is evoked for the object of this enmity, and I desire to seize the enemy. Yet I wish to keep this mystery, which I confide to thee alone, still hid from all the powers of heaven. Go thou, therefore, to the Virgin Mary. Pass thou on to that animate city whereof the prophet spoke in these words: 'Glorious things were spoken of thee, O city of God.' Proceed, then, to my rational paradise; proceed to the gate of the east; proceed to the place of sojourn that is worthy of my word; proceed to that second heaven on earth; proceed to the light cloud, and announce to it the shower of my coming; proceed to the sanctuary prepared for me; proceed to the hall of the incarnation; proceed to the pure chamber of my generation after the flesh. Speak in the ears of my rational ark, so as to prepare for me the accesses of hearing. But neither disturb nor vex the soul of the virgin. Manifest thyself in a manner befitting that sanctuary, and hail her first with the voice of gladness. And address Mary with the salutation, 'Hail, thou that art highly favored,' that I may show compassion for Eve in her depravation." The archangel heard these things, and considered them within himself, as was reasonable, and said: "Strange is this matter; passing comprehension is this thing that is spoken. He who is the object of dread to the cherubim, He who cannot be looked upon by the seraphim, He who is incomprehensible to all the heavenly powers, does He give the assurance of His connection with a maiden? does He announce His own personal coming? yea more, does He hold out an access by hearing? and is He who condemned Eve, urgent to put such honor upon her daughter? For He says: 'So as to prepare for me the accesses of hearing.' But can the womb contain Him who cannot be contained in space? Truly this is a dread mystery." While the angel is indulging such reflections, the Lord says to Him: "Why art thou troubled and perplexed, O Gabriel? Hast thou not already been sent by me to Zacharias the priest? Hast thou not conveyed to him the glad tidings of the nativity of John? Didst thou not inflict upon the incredulous priest the penalty of speechlessness? Didst thou not punish the aged man with dumbness? Didst thou not make thy declaration, and I confirmed it? And has not the actual fact followed upon thy announcement of good? Did not the barren woman conceive? Did not the womb obey the word? Did not the malady of sterility depart? Did not the inert disposition of nature take to flight? Is not she now one that shows fruitfulness, who before was never pregnant? Can anything be impossible with me, the Creator of all? Wherefore, then, art thou tossed with doubt?" What is the angel's answer to this? "O Lord," he says, "to remedy the defects of nature, to do away with the blast of evils, to recall the dead members to the power of life, to enjoin on nature the potency of generation, to remove barrenness in the case of members that have passed the common limit, to change the old and withered stalk into the appearance of verdant vigor, to set forth the fruitless soil suddenly as the producer of sheaves of corn,—to do all this is a work which, as it is ever the case, demands Thy power. And Sarah is a witness thereto, and along with her also Rebecca, and again Anna, who all, though bound by the dread ill of barrenness, were afterwards gifted by Thee with deliverance from that malady. But that a virgin should bring forth, without knowledge of a man, is something that goes beyond all the laws of nature; and dost Thou yet announce Thy coming to the maiden? The bounds of heaven and earth do not contain Thee, and how shall the womb of a virgin contain Thee?" And the Lord says: "How did the tent of Abraham contain me?" And the angel says: "As there were there the deeps of hospitality, O Lord, Thou didst show Thyself there to Abraham at the door of the tent, and didst pass quickly by it, as He who fills all things. But how can Mary sustain the fire of the divinity? Thy throne blazes with the illumination of its splendor, and can the virgin receive Thee without being consumed?" Then the Lord says: "Yea surely, if the fire in the wilderness injured the bush, my coming will indeed also injure Mary; but if that fire which served as the adumbration of the advent of the fire of divinity from heaven fertilized the bush, and did not burn it, what wilt thou say of the Truth that descends not in a flame of fire, but in the form of rain?" Thereupon the angel set himself to carry out the commission given him, and repaired to the Virgin, and addressed her with a loud voice, saying: "Hail, thou that are highly favored! the Lord is with thee. No longer shalt the devil be against thee; for where of old that adversary inflicted the wound, there now first of all does the Physician apply the salve of deliverance. Where death came forth, there has life now prepared its entrance. By a woman came the flood of our ills, and by a woman also our blessings have their spring. Hail, thou that are highly favored! Be not thou ashamed, as if thou wert the cause of our condemnation. For thou art made the mother of Him who is at once Judge and Redeemer. Hail, thou stainless mother of the Bridegroom of a world bereft! Hail, thou that hast sunk in thy womb the death (that came) of the mother (Eve)! Hail, thou animate temple of temple of God! Hail, thou equal home of heaven and earth alike! Hail, thou amplest receptacle of the illimitable nature!" But as these things are so, through her has come for the sick the Physician; for them that sit in darkness, the Sun of righteousness; for all that are tossed and tempest-beaten, the Anchor and the Port undisturbed by storm. For the servants in irreconcilable enmity has been born the Lord; and One has sojourned with us to be the bond of peace and the Redeemer of those led captive, and to be the peace for those involved in hostility. For He is our peace; and of that peace may it be granted that all we may receive the enjoyment, by the grace and kindness of our Lord Jesus Christ; to whom be the glory, honor, and power, now and ever, and unto all the ages of the ages. Amen.

The Fourth Homily.
On the Holy Theophany, or on Christ's Baptism.
O ye who are the friends of Christ, and the friends of the stranger, and the friends of the brethren, receive in kindness my speech to-day, and open your ears like the doors of hearing, and admit within them my discourse, and accept from me this saving proclamation of the baptism of Christ, which took place in the river

Jordan, in order that your loving desires may be quickened after the Lord, who has done so much for us in the way of condescension. For even though the festival of the Epiphany of the Savior is past, the grace of the same yet abides with us through all. Let us therefore enjoy it with insatiable minds; for insatiate desire is a good thing in the case of what pertains to salvation—yea, it is a good thing. Come therefore, all of us, from Galilee to Judea, and let us go forth with Christ; for blessed is he who journeys in such company on the way of life. Come, and with the feet of thought let us make for the Jordan, and see John the Baptist as he baptizes One who needs no baptism, and yet submits to the rite in order that He may bestow freely upon us the grace of baptism. Come, let us view the image of our regeneration, as it is emblematically presented in these waters. "Then cometh Jesus from Galilee to Jordan unto John, to be baptized of him." O how vast is the humility of the Lord! O how vast His condescension! The King of the heavens hastened to John, His own forerunner, without setting in motion the camps of His angels, without dispatching beforehand the incorporeal powers as His precursors; but presenting Himself in utmost simplicity, in soldier-like form, He comes up to His own subaltern. And He approached him as one of the multitude, and humbled Himself among the captives though He was the Redeemer, and ranged Himself with those under judgment though He was the Judge, and joined Himself with the lost sheep though He was the Good Shepherd who on account of the straying sheep came down from heaven, and yet did not forsake His heavens, and was mingled with the tares though He was that heavenly grain that springs unsown. And when the Baptist John then saw Him, recognizing Him whom before in his mother's womb he had recognized and worshipped, and discerning clearly that this was He on whose account, in a manner surpassing the natural time, he had leaped in the womb of his mother, in violation of the limits of nature, he drew his right hand within his double cloak, and bowing his head like a servant full of love to his master, addressed Him in these words: I have need to be baptized of Thee, and comes Thou to me? What is this Thou does, my Lord? Why dost Thou reverse the order of things? Why seek Thou along with the servants, at the hand of Thy servant, the things that are proper to servants? Why dost Thou desire to receive what Thou requires not? Why dost Thou burden me, Thy servitor, with Thy mighty condescension? I have need to be baptized of Thee, but Thou hast no need to be baptized of me. The less is blessed by the greater, and the greater is not blessed and sanctified by the less. The light is kindled by the sun, and the sun is not made to shine by the rush-lamp. The clay is wrought by the potter, and the potter is not molded by the clay. The creature is made anew by the Creator, and the Creator is not restored by the creature. The infirm is healed by the physician, and the physician is not cured by the infirm. The poor man receives contributions from the rich, and the rich borrow not from the poor. I have need to be baptized of Thee, and comes Thou to me? Can I be ignorant who Thou art, and from what source Thou hast Thy light, and whence Thou art come? Or, because Thou hast been born even as I have been, am I, then, to deny the greatness of Thy divinity? Or, because Thou hast condescended so far to me as to have approached my body, and dost bear me wholly in Thyself in order to effect the salvation of the whole man, am I, on account of that body of Thine which is seen, to overlook that divinity of Thine which is only apprehended? Or, because on behalf of my salvation Thou hast taken to Thyself the offering of my first fruits, am I to ignore the fact that Thou "covers Thyself with light as with a garment?" Or, because Thou wears the flesh that is related to me, and dost show Thyself to men as they are able to see Thee, am I to forget the brightness of Thy glorious divinity? Or, because I see my own form in Thee, am I to reason against Thy divine substance, which is invisible and incomprehensible? I know Thee, O Lord; I know Thee clearly. I know Thee, since I have been taught by Thee; for no one can recognize Thee, unless He enjoys Thine illumination. I know Thee, O Lord, clearly; for I saw Thee spiritually before I beheld this light. When Thou wert altogether in the incorporeal bosom of the heavenly Father, Thou wert also altogether in the womb of Thy handmaid and mother; and though held in the womb of Elisabeth by nature as in a prison and bound with the indissoluble bonds of the children unborn, leaped and celebrated Thy birth with anticipative rejoicings. Shall I then, who gave intimation of Thy sojourn on earth before Thy birth, fail to apprehend Thy coming after Thy birth? Shall I, who in the womb was a teacher of Thy coming, be now a child in understanding in view of perfect knowledge? But I cannot but worship Thee, who art adored by the whole creation; I cannot but proclaim Thee, of whom heaven gave the indication by the star, and for whom earth offered a kind reception by the wise men, while the choirs of angels also praised Thee in joy over Thy condescension to us, and the shepherds who kept watch by night hymned Thee as the Chief Shepherd of the rational sheep. I cannot keep silence while Thou art present, for I am a voice; yea, I am the voice, as it is said, of one crying in the wilderness, Prepare ye the way of the Lord. I have need to be baptized of Thee, and comes Thou to me? I was born, and thereby removed the barrenness of the mother that bore me; and while still a babe I became the healer of my father's speechlessness, having received of Thee from my childhood the gift of the miraculous. But Thou, being born of the Virgin Mary, as Thou didst will, and as Thou alone dost know, didst not do away with her virginity; but Thou didst keep it, and didst simply gift her with the name of mother: and neither did her virginity preclude Thy birth, nor did Thy birth injure her virginity. But these two things, so utterly opposite—bearing and virginity—harmonized with one intent; for such a thing abides possible with Thee, the Framer of nature. I am but a man and am a partaker of the divine grace; but Thou art God, and also man to the same effect: for Thou art by nature man's friend. I have need to be baptized of Thee, and comes Thou to me? Thou who was in the beginning, and was with God, and was God; Thou who art the brightness of the Father's glory; Thou who are the perfect image of the perfect Father; Thou who are the true light that lightened every man that cometh into the world; Thou who was in the world, and didst come where Thou was; Thou who was made flesh, and yet was not changed into the flesh; Thou who didst dwell among us, and didst manifest Thyself to Thy servants in the form of a servant; Thou who didst bridge earth and heaven together by Thy holy name,—comes Thou to me? One so great to such a one as I am? The King to the forerunner? The Lord to the servant? But though Thou was not ashamed to be born in the lowly measures of humanity, yet I have no ability to pass the measures of nature. I know how great is the measure of difference between earth and the Creator. I know how great is the distinction between the clay and the potter. I know how vast is the superiority possessed by Thee, who art the Sun of righteousness, over me who am but the torch of Thy grace. Even though Thou art compassed with the pure cloud of the body, I can still recognize Thy lordship. I acknowledge my own servitude, I proclaim Thy glorious greatness, I recognize Thy perfect lordship, I recognize my own perfect insignificance, I am not worthy to unloose the latchets of Thy shoes; and how shall I dare to touch Thy stainless head? How can I stretch out the right hand upon Thee, who didst stretch out the heavens like a curtain, and didst set the earth above the waters? How shall I spread those menial hands of mine upon Thy head? How shall I wash Thee, who art undefiled and sinless? How shall I enlighten the light? What manner of prayer shall I offer up over Thee, who dost receive the prayers even of those who are ignorant of Thee?

When I baptize others, I baptize into Thy name, in order that they may believe on Thee, who comes with glory; but when I baptize Thee, of whom shall I make mention? and into whose name shall I baptize Thee? Into that of the Father? But Thou hast the Father altogether in Thyself, and Thou art altogether in the Father. Or into that of the Son? But beside Thee there is no other Son of God by nature. Or into that of the Holy Spirit? But He is ever together with Thee, as being of one substance, and of one will, and of one judgment, and of one power, and of one honor with Thee; and He receives, along with Thee, the same adoration from all. Wherefore, O Lord, baptize Thou me, if Thou pleases; baptize me, the Baptist. Regenerate one whom Thou didst cause to be generated. Extend Thy dread right hand, which Thou hast prepared for Thyself, and crown my head by Thy touch, in order that I may run the course before Thy kingdom, crowned like a forerunner, and diligently announce the good tidings to the sinners, addressing them with this earnest call: "Behold the Lamb of God, that taketh away the sin of the world!" O river Jordan, accompany me in the joyous choir, and leap with me, and stir thy waters rhythmically, as in the movements of the dance; for thy Maker stands by thee in the body. Once of old didst thou see Israel pass through thee, and thou didst divide thy floods, and didst wait in expectation of the passage of the people; but now divide thyself more decidedly, and flow more easily, and embrace the stainless limbs of Him who at that ancient time did convey the Jews through thee. Ye mountains and hills, ye valleys and torrents, ye seas and rivers, bless the Lord, who has come upon the river Jordan; for through these streams He transmits sanctification to all streams. And Jesus answered and said to him: Suffer it to be so now, for thus it becometh us to fulfil all righteousness. Suffer it to be so now; grant the favor of silence, O Baptist, to the season of my economy. Learn to will whatever is my will. Learn to minister to me in those things on which I am bent, and do not pry curiously into all that I wish to do. Suffer it to be so now: do not yet proclaim my divinity; do not yet herald my kingdom with thy lips, in order that the tyrant may not learn the fact and give up the counsel he has formed with respect to me. Permit the devil to come upon me and enter the conflict with me as though I were but a common man, and receive thus his mortal wound. Permit me to fulfil the object for which I have come to earth. It is a mystery that is being gone through this day in the Jordan. My mysteries are for myself and my own. There is a mystery here, not for the fulfilling of my own need, but for the designing of a remedy for those who have been wounded. There is a mystery, which gives in these waters the representation of the heavenly streams of the regeneration of men. Suffer it to be so now: when thou sees me doing what seemed to me good among the works of my hands, in a manner befitting divinity, then attune thy praises to the acts accomplished. When thou sees me cleansing the lepers, then proclaim me as the framer of nature. When thou sees me make the lame ready runners, then with quickened pace do thou also prepare thy tongue to praise me. When thou sees me cast out demons, then hail my kingdom with adoration. When thou sees me raise the dead from their graves by my word, then, in concert with those thus raised, glorify me as the Prince of Life. When thou sees me on the Father's right hand, then acknowledge me to be divine, as the equal of the Father and the Holy Spirit, on the throne, and in eternity, and in honor. Suffer it to be so now; for thus it becometh us to fulfil all righteousness. I am the Lawgiver, and the Son of the Lawgiver; and it becometh me first to pass through all that is established, and then to set forth everywhere the intimations of my free gift. It becometh me to fulfil the law, and then to bestow grace. It becometh me to adduce the shadow, and then the reality. It becometh me to finish the old covenant, and then to dictate the new, and to write it on the hearts of men, and to subscribe it with my blood, and to seal it with my Spirit. It becometh me to ascend the cross, and to be pierced with its nails, and to suffer after the manner of that nature, which is capable of suffering, and to heal sufferings by my suffering, and by the tree to cure the wound that was inflicted upon men by the medium of a tree. It becometh me to descend even into the very depths of the grave, on behalf of the dead who are detained there. It becometh me, by my three days' dissolution in the flesh, to destroy the power of the ancient enemy, death. It becometh me to kindle the torch of my body for those who sit in darkness and in the shadow of death. It becometh me to ascend in the flesh to that place where I am in my divinity. It becometh me to introduce to the Father the Adam reigning in me. It be- cometh me to accomplish these things, for on account of these things I have taken my position with the works of my hands. It becometh me to be baptized with this baptism for the present, and afterwards to bestow the baptism of the consubstantial Trinity upon all men. Lend me, therefore, O Baptist, thy right hand for the present economy, even as Mary lent her womb for my birth. Immerse me in the streams of Jordan, even as she who bore me wrapped me in children's swaddling-clothes. Grant me thy baptism even as the Virgin granted me her milk. Lay hold of this head of mine, which the seraphim revere. With thy right-hand lay hold of this head, that is related to thyself in kinship. Lay hold of this head, which nature has made to be touched. Lay hold of this head, which for this very purpose has been formed by myself and my Father. Lay hold of this head of mine, which, if one does lay hold of it in piety, will save him from ever suffering shipwreck. Baptize me, who am destined to baptize those who believe on me with water, and with the Spirit, and with fire: with water, capable of washing away the defilement of sins; with the Spirit, capable of making the earthly spiritual; with fire, naturally fitted to consume the thorns of transgressions. On hearing these words, the Baptist directed his mind to the object of the salvation, and comprehended the mystery which he had received, and discharged the divine command; for he was at once pious and ready to obey. And stretching forth slowly his right hand, which seemed both to tremble and to rejoice, he baptized the Lord. Then the Jews who were present, with those in the vicinity and those from a distance, reasoned together, and spoke thus with themselves and with each other: Was it, then, without cause that we imagined John to be superior to Jesus? Was it without cause that we considered the former to be greater than the latter? Does not this very baptism attest the Baptist's pre-eminence? Is not he who baptized presented as the superior, and he who is baptized as the inferior? But while they, in their ignorance of the mystery of the economy, babbled in such wise with each other, He who alone is Lord, and by nature the Father of the Only-begotten, He who alone knows perfectly Him whom He alone in passionless fashion begat, to correct the erroneous imaginations of the Jews, opened the gates of the heavens, and sent down the Holy Spirit in the form of a dove, lighting upon the head of Jesus, pointing out thereby the new Noah, yea the maker of Noah, and the good pilot of the nature which is in shipwreck. And He Himself calls with clear voice out of heaven, and says: "This is my beloved Son,"—the Jesus there, namely, and not the John; the one baptized, and not the one baptizing; He who was begotten of me before all periods of time and not he who was begotten of Zacharias; He who was born of Mary after the flesh, and not he who was brought forth by Elisabeth beyond all expectation; He who was the fruit of the virginity yet preserved intact, and not he who was the shoot from a sterility removed; He who has had His conversation with you, and not he who was brought up in the wilderness. This is my beloved Son, in whom I am well pleased: my Son, of the same substance with myself, and not of a different; of one substance with me according to what is unseen, and of one substance with you according to what is seen, yet without sin. This is He who along with me made man. This is my beloved Son, in whom I am well pleased. This Son of mine and this son of Mary are not two distinct persons; but this is my beloved Son,—this one who is both seen with the eye and apprehended with the mind. This is my beloved Son, in whom I am well pleased; hear Him. If He shall say, I and my Father are one, hear Him. If He shall say, He that hath seen me hath seen the Father, hear Him. If He shall say, He that hath sent me is greater than I, adapt the voice to the economy. If He shall say, Whom do men say that I the Son of man am? answer ye Him thus: Thou art the Christ, the Son of the living God. By these words, as they were sent from the Father out of heaven in thunder-form, the race of men was enlightened: they ap- prehended the difference between the Creator and the creature, between the King and the soldier (subject), between the Worker and the work; and being strengthened in faith, they drew near through the baptism of John to Christ, our true God, who baptized with the Spirit and with fire. To Him be glory, and to the Father, and to the most holy and quickening Spirit, now and ever, and unto the ages of the ages. Amen.

Elucidations.

I can do no better than follow Dupin as to the authorship of these Homilies. He thinks the style of

Proclus (of Constantinople) may be detected in them, though the fourth is beyond him for eloquence, and has even been thought worthy of St. Chrysostom. It was produced after Nicæa, and probably after Ephesus, its somewhat exaggerated praises of the θεοτόκος being unusual at an earlier period. The titles of these Homilies are the work of much later editors; and interpolations probably occur frequently, by the same hands.

On All the Saints.

Grant thy blessing, Lord.

It was my desire to be silent, and not to make a public display of the rustic rudeness of my tongue. For silence is a matter of great consequence when one's speech is mean. And to refrain from utterance is indeed an admirable thing, where there is lack of training; and verily he is the highest philosopher who knows how to cover his ignorance by abstinence from public address. Knowing, therefore, the feebleness of tongue proper to me, I should have preferred such a course. Nevertheless the spectacle of the onlookers impels me to speak. Since then, this solemnity is a glorious one among our festivals, and the spectators form a crowded gathering, and our assembly is one of elevated fervor in the faith, I shall face the task of commencing an address with confidence. And this I may attempt all the more boldly, since the Father requests me, and the Church is with me, and the sainted martyrs with this object strengthen what is weak in me. For these have inspired aged men to accomplish with much love a long course and constrained them to support their failing steps by the staff of the word; and they have stimulated women to finish their course like the young men, and have brought to this, too, those of tender years, yea, even creeping children. In this wise have the martyrs shown their power, leaping with joy in the presence of death, laughing at the sword, making sport of the wrath of princes, grasping at death as the producer of deathlessness, making victory their own by their fall, through the body taking their leap to heaven, suffering their members to be scattered abroad in order that they might hold their souls, and, bursting the bars of life, that they might open the gates of heaven. And if anyone believes not that death is abolished, that Hades is trodden under foot, that the chains thereof are broken, that the tyrant is bound, let him look on the martyrs disporting themselves in the presence of death, and taking up the jubilant strain of the victory of Christ. O the marvel! Since the hour when Christ despoiled Hades, men have danced in triumph over death. "O death, where is thy sting! O grave, where is thy victory?" Hades and the devil have been despoiled, and stripped of their ancient armor, and cast out of their peculiar power. And even as Goliath had his head cut off with his own sword, so also is the devil, who has been the father of death, put to rout through death; and he finds that the selfsame thing which he was wont to use as the ready weapon of his deceit, has become the mighty instrument of his own destruction. Yea, if we may so speak, casting his hook at the Godhead, and seizing the wonted enjoyment of the baited pleasure, he is himself manifestly caught while he deems himself the captor, and discovers that in place of the man he has touched the God. By reason thereof do the martyrs leap upon the head of the dragon, and despise every species of torment. For since the second Adam has brought up the first Adam out of the deeps of Hades, as Jonah was delivered out of the whale, and has set forth him who was deceived as a citizen of heaven to the shame of the deceiver, the gates of Hades have been shut, and the gates of heaven have been opened, so as to offer an unimpeded entrance to those who rise thither in faith. In olden time Jacob beheld a ladder erected reaching to heaven, and the angels of God ascending and descending upon it. But now, having been made man for man's sake, He who is the Friend of man has crushed with the foot of His divinity him who is the enemy of man, and has borne up the man with the hand of His Christhood, and has made the trackless ether to be trodden by the feet of man. Then the angels were ascending and descending; but now the Angel of the great counsel neither ascended nor descended: for whence or where shall He change His position, who is present everywhere, and fills all things, and holds in His hand the ends of the world? Once, indeed,

He descended, and once He ascended,—not, however, through any change of nature, but only in the condescension of His philanthropic Christhood;[604] and He is seated as the Word with the Father, and as the Word He dwells in the womb, and as the Word He is found everywhere, and is never separated from the God of the universe. Aforetime did the devil deride the nature of man with great laughter, and he has had his joy over the times of our calamity as his festal days. But the laughter is only a three days' pleasure, while the wailing is eternal; and his great laughter has prepared for him a greater wailing and ceaseless tears, and inconsolable weeping, and a sword in his heart. This sword did our Leader forge against the enemy with fire in the virgin furnace, in such wise and after such fashion as He willed, and gave it its point by the energy of His invincible divinity, and dipped it in the water of an undefiled baptism, and sharpened it by sufferings without passion in them, and made it bright by the mystical resurrection; and herewith by Himself He put to death the vengeful adversary, together with his whole host. What manner of word, therefore, will ex- press our joy or his misery? For he who was once an archangel is now a devil; he who once lived in heaven is now seen crawling like a serpent upon earth; he who once was jubilant with the cherubim, is now shut up in pain in the guard-house of swine; and him, too, in fine, shall we put to rout if we mind those things which are contrary to his choice, by the grace and kindness of our Lord Jesus Christ, to whom be the glory and the power unto the ages of the ages. Amen.

Elucidations.

The feast of *All Saints* is very ancient in the Oriental churches, and is assigned to the *Octave of Pentecost*, the Anglican Trinity Sunday. See Neale, *Eastern Church*, vol. ii. pp. 734, 753. In the West it was instituted when Boniface III. (who accepted from the Emperor Phocas the title of "Universal Bishop," a.d. 607) turned the Pantheon into a church, and with a sort of practical epigram called it the church of "All the Saints." It was a local festival until the ninth century, when the Emperor Louis the Pious introduced it into France and Germany. Thence it came to England. It falls on the 1st of November.

The gates of the church at Rome are the same which once opened for the worship of "all the gods." They are of massive bronze, and are among the most interesting of the antiquities of the city.

The modern gates of St. Peter's, at Rome, are offensive copies of heathen mythology; and among the subjects there represented, is the shameful tale of Leda,— a symbol of the taste of Leo X.

On the Gospel According to Matthew

(Chapter VI. 22, 23.)
"The light of the body is the eye: if therefore thine eye be single, thy whole body shall be full of light. But if thine eye be evil, thy whole body shall be full of darkness. If therefore the light that is in thee be darkness, how great is that darkness!"

The single eye is the love unfeigned; for when the body is enlightened by it, it sets forth through the medium of the outer members only things which are perfectly correspondent with the inner thoughts. But the evil eye is the pretended love, which is also called hypocrisy, by which the whole body of the man is made darkness. We have to consider that deeds meet only for darkness may be within the man, while through the outer members he may produce words that seem to be of the light: for there are those who are in reality wolves, though they may be covered with sheep's clothing. Such are they who wash only the outside of the cup and platter, and do not understand that, unless the inside of these things is cleansed, the outside itself cannot be made pure. Wherefore, in manifest confutation of such persons, the Savior says: "If the light that is in thee be darkness, how great is that darkness!" That is to say, if the love which seems to thee to be light is really a work meet for darkness, by reason of some hypocrisy concealed in thee, what must be thy patent transgressions!

Find this and other great works of the early Church Fathers at lighthousechristianpublishing.com.

Our Father who art in heaven, hallowed be
thy name.
Thy kingdom come, Thy will be done, on
earth as it is in heaven.
Give us this day our daily bread and
forgive us our trespasses as we forgive those who
trespass against us.
And lead us not into temptation, but deliver
us from evil, for Thy is the kingdom, the power
and the glory.

Amen

Gregory Thaumaturgus

Hail Mary full of grace, the Lord is with thee. Blessed art thou amongst women and blessed is the fruit of thy womb Jesus. Holy Mary mother of God, pray for us sinners, now and the hour of our death.

www.ingramcontent.com/pod-product-compliance
Lightning Source LLC
Chambersburg PA
CBHW052141070526
44585CB00017B/1921